I0082279

Author's Note

This book is for entertainment purposes. It is not intended as a substitute for psychological or psychiatric counseling or other medical advice. Please consult with a qualified medical professional for any individual health or medical-related counsel. Nikki Nokes is not licensed in the practice of psychology, social work or psychiatry. Further, in no way should anything contained in this book be construed as legal advice or counseling. Any references to specific individuals contained in this book have been disguised to protect their privacy. All research and information was gathered via formal and informal interviews with individuals posed the question "What do women do or not do, think or not think that keeps them single?"

An Inkspiration Press Book
Published by Inkspiration Press

First Paperback Edition: February 2010
Library of Congress Control Number: 2009943986
ISBN-13: 978-0-9817922-0-0
ISBN-10: 0-9817922-0-0

Book and cover designed by April Carter Grant
Typography (main body text): Times New Roman
Author Photo: Frederic Charpentier

Manufactured in the United States of America.

www.inkspirationpress.com | www.nikkinokes.com

Maybe... It's You!™

INKSPIRATION PRESS
LOS ANGELES

Contents

Acknowledgments

I'd like to dedicate this book to my friends and family for their support and encouragement and especially for their suspension of disbelief when I announced that I was going to "write a book."

Thank you to Mom and Dad for the great edu-ma-cation that allows me to express my thoughts.

Thank you to my grandmother, Nana, for the good advice, the many laughs and my name.

Thank you to April Carter Grant for the book layout and design. Here's to getting one more project in the can. You're an excellent mind-reader!

Thank you to my girlfriends for early reviews of my writing and for your candid and thoughtful feedback. Special thanks to Danielle, Kathleen and Allison. You didn't have to, but you did; and I appreciate you for it.

And finally, thank you to all for excusing the unreturned phone calls and missed social engagements. Hopefully you'll appreciate the fruit of my labors.

DISCLAIMER
While I am a lawyer by profession, I am not a doctor or psychologist. I do not profess that my advice should in any way be interpreted as a medical or professional opinion. It should be taken with a swig of your favorite martini, just like the words of any of your other girlfriends, of course, only if you're of legal drinking age.

-NN

Introduction

I love the concept of a book's "introduction." Not only do I get the opportunity to "introduce" this book's topic to you, but I also get the opportunity to introduce myself. Most likely, we've never personally met, but you know me just the same. I'm your "tell it like it is" tough-love girlfriend. When you finally decide you're not afraid to hear the truth, I'm the one with the difficult job of holding up a mirror and calling you out on your b-s. Don't we all need someone, even if it's just one girlfriend, who will tell us honestly when we really do look fat in that dress?! I guess as hard as the truth is to hear at times, it is even harder to dole out to those that you love for fear of hurting feelings and deflating egos. Well, someone's gotta do the dirty work!

Girlfriend, we're taking an amazing journey together! We're starting a new conversation – one that does not center specifically on "men are dogs." We've had that discussion before – so many times! This is all about us – from one girlfriend to another, getting down and dirty with the truth about ourselves and how we contribute to our own singleness. Like you, I've dealt with the struggles of being a single woman, not just in her 20's, but into her 30's as well. Believe me, I know, it's a rough place to be. I've had more than my fair share of disappointments. I've had the one that almost was, but wasn't; the one that stomped on my feelings; the one that cheated on me with my friend; and of course, the one that just stopped calling for no reason… the week before Christmas. Girlfriend, you talk about dating drama, ugh! I've been through it all!

I got the idea for writing this book because I got tired. I got tired of being told that he doesn't like me, or if he did like me he would act differently. I wanted more. I desperately wanted a ray of hope, something to say when inevitably someone remarked, "But I can't believe you're still single!" Isn't that the worst? If <u>you</u> can't believe I'm still single, imagine how I feel!

That being single frustration most often surfaced in conversations with the girls, usually over drinks. No matter what we're talking about, from climate change to our favorite shoe designers, the ultimate focus of the discussion has eventually landed on men and relationships. It's taken different tones, "men are dogs," "men are stupid," "men don't listen," "men cheat," "men lie" and any combination or iteration of that list, plus more. If you and your other girlfriends are anything like me and mine, you know exactly what I'm talking about!

What I started to notice is while we easily spent our time discussing what was wrong with "them," the conversation never really turned to "us" with an honest critique of what we might be doing that contributed to the results we were getting out of our relationships. We never shared advice and expectations for better experiences. This thought evolved into "Maybe It's You."

Maybe It's You is a self-empowerment tool for the single girlfriends to not only spark a personal, internal dialogue, but also a new type of conversation amongst each other, this time, one that might lead to a new and different conclusion and ultimately a different result other than, men suck and I'm still single.

Maybe It's You is an attempt to answer the question, "why." Why is he not into me? Why doesn't he commit to me? Why am I not meeting anyone? Why am I still single?? Hopefully, Girlfriend, the answer is in the pages that follow.

I started this book as a tool for myself. I'm not approaching this topic from the perspective of someone who has it all figured out. You're a traveler venturing with me in the quest for my very own "why." I'm not the all-knowing elder perched on high, showering down words of innate wisdom while wildly waving my blinged-out left ring finger in everyone's face. I am part of this book's audience: a single and fabulous girlfriend, making her way, wanting to have it all and trying to figure it all out. I am also the social scientist, the observer, who believes that asking enough people the right questions is the best path to the complete truth. Is this book the Wikipedia of dating? No. But, it is the condensed version of the survey responses of hundreds of people, men and women, who were asked to name the culprit: "What is it that women do, or don't do; think or don't think that keeps them single?"

The responses I got were a wake-up call to me, Girlfriend; a clear, ringing confirmation that not only do I not have it all figured out, but I also have so very much to work on. My being single is in part because of statistics and circumstances. But, it is also a result of my unthinking behaviors. Of this, I am now certain. The same may be true for you.

Trust me that the information that follows is as challenging as it is insightful. Reading this book will require courage as well as a healthy dose of curiosity. Taking the steps to master yourself and your relationships, well, *that* is going to take determination, understanding, perseverance, and most certainly, the support and encouragement of your girlfriends.

I don't pretend to have all the answers, but I set out to get them. Here, I share them with you in the hopes that as I continue my quest for the "why," by discovering the answer to that pesky question, both you and I can also find increased success in our personal, romantic relationships.

We all deserve to be happy, Girlfriend. Sometimes, it just takes a little work. So, with that, I pose to you the following question, if you are single, have you ever considered… maybe it's you?

Basically, Maybe It's You...

MIY Maybe you don't listen.

I know by now you've figured out that this is going to be some "tough love" coming your way. I am personally a fan of "tell it like it is" tough love because it is that brand of realness that identifies the direct location of the weak spots in your armor. It highlights your vulnerabilities. The only problem is, those spots are sensitive! But like a wound that won't heal, sometimes you have to rip off the scab and air that festering nasty thing out! And so it is with your issues that may be keeping you single. It's hard to have the finger pointed at you, whether by me or another girlfriend or even guys that you've dated. All criticism is challenging to receive, even if constructive and especially if it's to the point. Poking on a sensitive and vulnerable area can and often does hurt. That said, it's the best thing that can happen to you. If the criticism is not applicable, rather than jump to your own defense, what harm is it to think for a moment? Instead of a knee-jerk, "That's not me!", why not take the time to consider, "Maybe it is me…"? Are you worried that you might actually find some area for improvement? Too many of the girlfriends rush to their own defense entirely too quickly when confronted with criticism. Girlfriend, when you're talking, you're not listening. It's a fact. So, if someone is doing you the favor of pointing out a potential flaw in your personality or actions, and you rush to defend yourself, you completely miss what's being said. And what they're telling you, if true, could be a priceless piece of information to act on. If it's not applicable, then you're free to disregard it. There's no judge and jury here, just you. So no need to play your own defense attorney. Simply take the information and process it. If it's worthless, throw it in your mental trash can; but if it's valuable, do your best to act on it. Defensive girlfriends are single!

I remember something a guy told me once when

giving me my own measure of "constructive criticism." Of course, as he was telling me about a particular thing that I was not doing, I rushed to my own defense. As he started to become frustrated, he took a step back and said, "You know, I realize what I'm saying could feel like an attack. It's not. This is like me telling you in a baseball game that one of your bases is open. Instead of taking a look at the field, while you spend the time telling me which ones you have covered, the runner is stealing home." Girlfriend, don't let the runner steal home and keep you single!

Not being able to deal with criticism is a huge issue that keeps many of the girlfriends single. As a result, the conversation devolves into a "men suck" discussion that gets us nowhere. Where does "men suck" ultimately lead – it leads to the final conclusion "men suck." Awesome. Just great. What do we do with that? We should hope there is something we can personally work on in our thoughts or actions that might, if investigated further, improve our experience in dating. You should be begging for criticism. You should hope there is something that you can address within yourself. That, my proactive Girlfriend, is something you can control. The key to being able to accept criticism is to realize you're only the person you are today just this one day in your entire life. Tomorrow is a new day and with it comes a new you. Each moment carries the opportunity to change yourself for the better. Change doesn't have to happen all at once, either. It can happen in little tiny adjustments until you get there.

Find a way to deal with criticism even if it means you have to discipline yourself to write it down before you respond. Every non-positive comment involving you is not an attack. Try dropping the weapons first and listen before you mount your defense.

A WORD ABOUT *too much criticism...*

Ultimately too much flaw-finding can be a toxic experience for anyone. If it's your guy, he should like you as much for the person you are as he does for the person you could be. As a general rule, accept constructive criticism only from those people you trust with your well-being. And everything you listen to doesn't have to be something you accept as true. It's all just information we are giving you, Girlfriend, in the hopes that it is helpful. By all means, if it doesn't apply (and most likely, some of it won't) let it go. Or, share it with someone else!

MIY Maybe, you don't know what you want.

Let's say you've been saving for 10 years and you now have $5000 with the single objective to buy a car. Do you just keep riding your bicycle until you see any old rusty junk-bucket automobile with a $5000 price tag? Would you just plunk down your hard-earned cash hoping that sucker starts and you can ride off into the sunset? I think not Girlfriend! Most likely, you would at least set some basic standards you require for any car you're going to purchase with your money. Unless you own a junkyard, or curate an automotive museum, first things first, you want that nice, healthy rumbling hum when the key hits the ignition. You want it to have all four tires and no flats. You want it to have a decent paint job and an engine in good condition. Come to think of it, you probably want to make sure the interior is not too worn and the radio works. And the more you think about this car, all sorts of qualifications should be coming to mind about what you would need, especially if you're going to spend your last dime on it.

Given that this book is not a guide to car-buying, but rather guy-getting, I think you probably know where I'm headed here. This car analogy is representative of you, my single Girlfriend, and your dating life. You've put all the time, focus and attention into becoming the person you are, and you're looking to share this wonderfully developed person with someone else, but to no success. Sure, some near misses, but the much desired goal still eludes you. Well, Girlfriend, sometimes the biggest obstacles are those most obvious, yet most difficult to identify. Here's what I propose. How can you expect to not be single, when you don't know what kind of person you want to be with? How can you be sure you're getting what you need when you haven't figured out what works for you? Unfortunately, men don't fall under the "Lemon Laws" like cars do. If you make a bad choice, sometimes, you're just stuck with the clunker of a guy you've got, and that might be even worse than being alone. From my experience, my surveys, and just general common sense basics, the number one problem the Girlfriends have when it comes to chronic singledom is an absolute failure to define what you want.

(Dramatic Pause)

And here it comes in 5…4…3…2…1, by now the thought has likely popped into your mind, "Ohmygod! I really have *no* idea what I want! How can I define what I want if I'm clueless about it?" Stress ye not. So very many of my disappointed, disgruntled and delusional girlfriends tell me about their failed relationships with the various varieties of Man X, including what a jerk he is and how he didn't do this, that and the next thing, to which I say, "Yes, that does suck, but what did you want from the beginning?" And to my question, even my most clueless girlfriend at minimum replies, " All I do know is I didn't want *that*!" So I say to you, if you've been paying attention to your own experiences, you do know what you want – even if right now it only amounts to knowing what you don't want. All you need is a starting place. Start with what you don't want and let that inspire you to begin defining what you do want.

This will come up later, but Girlfriend, as you start thinking and defining, you don't want to get too specific. What does that mean? Rather than laser focusing on particular objective criteria (*e.g.*, height, income, looks, etc.), when you're thinking about what you want, get to the root of what's important, and that's ultimately how that person is going to make you *feel*. Want an example? Let's say you tell yourself, I don't want a guy who is shorter than me. But, maybe it's not the feet and inches height thing specifically. Maybe it's something else. Maybe you don't want a guy shorter than you because: (1)

you think that people will look at you funny; and (2) you're a little self-conscious, so the extra attention you perceive from people looking at the two of you together would make you uncomfortable. If that's the case, is his height really the issue? Isn't that more a *you* thing? I actually have a girlfriend who is literally scared of short men. For her, this is really a deal-breaker. But, short of having a true phobia (no pun intended here), reconsider and get to the real deal core issue of what it is you really want. You want a guy that makes you feel like a glamazon when you're together. Someone who you feel compliments you and makes you feel safe and protected. Someone you don't mind wearing your $500 stilettos with because what he contributes to your life makes him seem like the tallest man in the world and makes you feel like a supermodel.

So, instead of getting stuck on those little pesky superficial qualities, get down and dirty about your true wants and needs. Start thinking about what that person is supposed to add to your life. Need some help? I thought you might. That's why I've included a table of some of the most common superficial qualities I've heard my girlfriends list off to me and I've taken the liberty of drilling down a bit on those to what the real desire might be. Once you think about it on your own, it will start to make a lot of sense.

Hey, Girlfriend! CHECK THIS OUT

She Says...	She Means...
Tall	Compliments me physically. Makes me feel secure and protected. Makes me feel glamorous with him as part of a couple.
Smart	Can engage in great conversations. Knows more than me about certain topics I find interesting. Can find his way out of a paper bag.
Handsome (has all his hair, and the like)	I personally find him so attractive that other people's thoughts and opinions don't matter. I'm just too happy to care.
Good Job	Happy and fulfilled with what he's doing with his life. Has found a way to financially support himself and to play the role I need him to play in our courtship (whether it be dinners or travel or gifts or whatever) and ultimately our relationship.
Buys Me Expensive Gifts	Makes me feel appreciated, like a veritable princess. Goes out of his way to do special things for me, exactly what I'd like, and exactly how I'd like it.
Good Credit	Can buy, do and have whatever he wants (and maybe what I want and/or need too).
Ambitious	He sets and accomplishes goals. Better yet, he sets and accomplishes the right goals at the right time for his own personal growth and development. He's constantly striving to become a better all-around person.
Matching Race or Ethnicity	Speaks the same cultural language. "Gets me" and won't be turned off by my crazy family.
Has a Big ______	Ok, well...there's really no substitute for that is there? Just to make an attempt (because I did promise)... pleases and satisfies me physically. Comfortably opens me up to new sexual experiences. Makes me feel like a goddess rockstar pornstar sensuous all-out sexy beastlady!

See? Despite the general awesomeness of the Superman-like, yet entirely superficial left-hand side qualities, you probably connect more with the descriptions listed in the right-hand column. Even more, the descriptions in the right column paint a clearer picture of who you might be looking for than the left side. And here's the funny thing, if I gave you the choice of two guys, the first that meets all the criteria in the right column and the second that meets all of the criteria in the left, the first guy may not be an exact match for ANY of those qualities in the left column, but I bet dollars to doughnuts you'd rather have him, hands down because you'd be getting someone much closer to what it is you really do want. Those objective criteria are just a guessing game. All they do is serve to limit your dating options… and… keep you single.

Girlfriend, you need to figure out what you *want*! Put this book down, and grab some paper and a pen. Maybe pop in an old *Sex and the City* episode, one where the dating actually goes right – so that means, only watch the first half. Get some inspiration from a romantic comedy movie or a soap opera. Don't pay attention to the superficial qualities of the main guy, but start trying to figure out what it is about him and the impact that he has on the female lead (and you watching) that makes him so attractive and desirable. Then, take that inspiration and start really focusing on yourself to write your own description! What do you want to feel? What would make you happy? New adventures? Constant laughing and smiling? Feeling like a treasure? Feeling safe and protected? Get to writing!

MIY Maybe you want to be single and are in denial about it.

Girlfriend, there is absolutely nothing wrong with wanting to be single. The problem comes when you don't realize it or are in dating denial. Denial is a rushing river that has drowned many a girlfriend. For example? I have this one girlfriend, she says "I know for a fact I want to wind up with a guy that has quality X. It's like the most important thing to me, and it's totally a dealbreaker." If you were paying attention earlier, you should be saying to yourself, "but shouldn't she be focusing on less absolute and less superficial qualities?" And to this I say, certainly, yes she should... unless... she actually *wants* to be single. And if she wanted to be single, she'd hold on very tightly to absolute criteria and then pursue only guys that didn't possess those characteristics. And that's exactly what this girlfriend did. One after another, she steadily pursued guys who had qualities A-Z, but never, the oh-so important quality X. It got to a point that I actually asked her in a conversation why, if she knew she wanted quality X, she wasn't making that the first thing she went for. After a long pause, she said… "Well, maybe it's because I'm really not ready to be in a relationship." Aha!

Let me give you a little bit more information about this girlfriend. She had recently moved to a new city for a new job. Several of her investments were in trouble and she was in the process of righting the wrongs of a bad economy. She had plenty of friends generally, but was still getting to know not only people in her new city, but also, in her workplace. All told, she was in a place of personal discomfort. Being uncomfortable, either with yourself or with your personal situation is more than enough reason to play it solo for the immediate moment until things calm down a bit. And that's exactly what this girlfriend was doing, but subconsciously. Consciously, her fabulous overactive mind was steadily wondering, "Why am I not connecting with anyone?"

Life is already complicated and we've all got so much

to figure out: what we want to do, how are we going to get there, how are we going to pay for it and more. It's enough to make your head spin. The road to developing yourself is a long, difficult one and at times, it warrants being alone to figure it all out. Even more, after a trauma or something that's got you out of sorts, you just don't have the emotional energy to deal with another person and their drama. You don't want to take the time to figure it or them out because right now, it's gotta be all about you. And that's ok… if that's what you need and you're being honest with yourself about it. But then, if that were actually the case, you wouldn't exactly be reading this book would you?

When you subconsciously want to be single, you'll unknowingly play any number of little games with yourself – going after guys you know are unavailable or generally wrong, just as long as it's pretty much a certainty you could never have a future with them or bring them around your parents. You know these guys – they are the ones that even you don't know what you see in them. And yet, if you're wasting your time with them, unless you're insane, or have some other issue way beyond the scope of this book, you're probably doing it because you really truly deep down want to be single; you just don't think you should want to be single. Rather than to waste your time with a big loser on the road to nowhere, break free Girlfriend!! Handle what needs to be handled in your own life and save your energy for someone really worth it. In fact, the time and focus that you're wasting on Mr. Wrong is just extending the process of resolving whatever is necessary so you can start being available to Mr. Right. Get your chips off the roulette table! Focus your attention and your energies! If you're going to bet, put it all on Girlfriend #1, you!

Take inventory of who you've been meeting and/or dating. Are they far outside of who you could ultimately envision yourself winding up with? You don't have to marry every guy you meet, but every guy that you consider dating should be available to you. At minimum, available to you for the same things and in the same way that you're available to him. If that's not the case, and you're still lustfully pursuing him, maybe your really wanting to be single is the culprit. Do yourself the favor and examine the open items in your life that have nothing to do with romance, but rather finance, your home, your job, your surroundings and your basic level of comfort. Are there some pressing unresolved issues screaming for your attention? If so, stop. Take a breather and tie up your lose ends. No sense in forcing yourself into dating when all your subconscious is going to do is push you in the opposite direction.

MIY Maybe you're a control freak.

My modern day Girlfriend! Isn't it wonderful that we can think, be, do and have whatever we want? How fabulous is it that the only thing standing between you and your heart's desires is some good old fashioned hard work? What magnificent freedom! Right? When you're dating? Um, no. Unfortunately, believe it or not, it just may be this exact mindset, "I can get whatever I want if I just put in the work," that is keeping you single. Inside and outside of our work environments, we are control freaks! If you can order your coffee as a medium, extra hot, no foam, two pump, sugar-free vanilla soy latte in a small cup, you'd like to be able to be as particular about your man, his timing and his behavior, right? Well, all I can say to that is, it's nice to want things.

It's too bad that dating, when it involves a potential relationship with another person, doesn't work like a Starbucks menu! The early stages of a new relationship, that time when you first meet a new guy, is the time the relationship is the most fragile. He doesn't know you from Adam, or Eve, and the bulk of your actions and behaviors he's interpreting with no context and thus based on past experiences. To him, you're not "you" yet, so he's still viewing you as an average woman, which is a concept he's developed based on his previous interactions with other women. If you're over-aggressive, to him, before he knows how you think and respond and how rational you really are, your actions start to look like that psycho chick he had to change his phone number to get rid of last year! So, when you haven't heard from him for a day or two, and you're just calling to say "Hi!", especially after the third (or thirtieth) time, despite your innocent intentions, that may really say to him, "Run! She's crazy!" Why take that risk when you don't have to?

While he should immediately realize the totality of your awesomeness and right away do everything within his power to establish your constant presence in his life, it might take him a little bit of time. Initially, he's just feeling things out, getting a sense of his bearings with you, and trying to understand you as a person. If you know you'd like to move things forward, too often, we try to force progress, taking the reins from this slow-moving, seemingly passive man, kick the horse in the haunches and expect to bring that slow trot to a canter. Girlfriend, you're going to have to relax! First off, if he's not calling you, his fingers are not broken, his phone service hasn't been terminated, he hasn't lost your number and he's not waiting for you to call him. It is the rare man who does not go for exactly what he wants. It's the thrill of overcoming the challenge (why do you think they like video games so much!). In fact, many of them, if they <u>really</u> like you, are so persistent that you might have to beat them off with a stick! They just don't know when to give it up! I'm sure you've had that guy at least once in your life. What you want to avoid, Girlfriend, is becoming the equivalent of "that guy" to your brand-new man in your just-recently established relationship.

What you also don't want to do, besides be a generally unwelcome presence, is come across as too aggressive to be chased. The idea is you should be easy to find, but not that easy to get! If you seem like a low-hanging fruit, he's not going to appreciate you for the work it took to get you. Besides putting him off, you'll also never know how hard he's willing to work to keep you. Sometimes, there is just nothing for you to do, but wait. Girlfriend, I know. We all hate to wait. We want it now, right away and there's got to be something we can do about it to make it happen. Well, this might work when you're at the coffee shop and the line is too long, but it does not work in relationships. That guy doesn't want to be rushed. He wants to call you on his own time, when he wants and how he wants. Dating you should feel to him like his decision. To that end, you can't decide for him when the two of you are going to speak. Once you make your preferences known, it's up to you to give him the time and latitude to figure out on his own how to meet them. You can tell him what, but you cannot and must not tell him how. The desires that you do communicate get translated by your guy as absolutes, even if you don't mean it that way. Guys don't do gray, just black and white. Since you're already telling him "what" to do, if you're also telling him "how" you want things done, you start to become an ultimatum-spouting irritation rather than a devastating enigma that he must figure out and capture.

Finally, my over-eager Girlfriend, don't try to anticipate his wants and needs. Just be yourself and let things flow in a natural course. Don't try to be his mother, lover, sister, entertainment, doctor and best friend all at once in the first days or weeks of meeting him. Eventually with time, you will grow to be those things for each other. Of course, if your guy is like most men, it will seem to you like he's living in the dark ages and you can't wait to get that toilet-paper holder for his bathroom (or toilet paper, if he's really living foul). The truth is, when you first met him, he existed perfectly fine on his own with probably an ample cache of resources to help him make it through life. So, hold off - let him come to you and gauge his temperature for your intervention with gentle (you see this word, *gentle* right?) suggestions or inquiries. See if he actually does want or need your help. If he says he doesn't, believe him. Chances are, he's not just being macho and he's not just embarrassed to admit he needs assistance. He *honestly believes* he doesn't need the emergency intervention you've been planning; so until he changes his mind (on his own), don't you try to do it for him. He's not going to hold it against you later, and you'll show him your relevance to his life in other ways not involving taking over responsibility for his survival. He's going to be alright. Trust me.

Like I said at the very beginning, this book is not intended to tell you when a guy doesn't like you. It's intended to keep you from running off a guy that might like you until you went crazy control-freak psycho-chick on him! Listen, you have to be comfortable with what men call "the Silence." During the Silence, he doesn't talk and neither should you. Nor should you feel that either you or he need to speak. It doesn't mean that he doesn't like you or find you entertaining; it just means that you don't have to play an active role in his life at that very moment. The Silence can also, and most often does, involve him not calling. Girlfriend, most men do not like to talk on the phone! That doesn't mean they won't; it just means if he is calling, it's probably because he knows you want him to. So, don't stop breathing if he hasn't called you for 24 hours. Learn how to exist in the Silence. It's good practice for being comfortable when you two are actually in a defined relationship and the Silence involves more things than him just not using the phone. To help you recognize and deal with the Silence, I've taken the liberty of highlighting several delusions we girlfriends often adopt when we aren't in active communication with our guy. Take these as facts. When you find yourself in the Silence, repeat them to yourself until you accept them as truth and put the phone down. Whatever you do, do not call him!

Hey, Girlfriend! CHECK THIS OUT

Reasons Not to Call Him

1. Men do exactly what they want to do.

2. He did not lose your number.

3. His fingers are not broken.

4. He is not waiting for you to call him.

5. He is not wondering if he should ask you out because he thinks you'll say no. [So you should not just let him know (again) that you had a great time on the first date and you can't wait to see him.].

6. He is not too shy to call you (especially if he's already called you once).

7. He has not forgotten how to speak English.

8. He has not been in an accident, nor is he in the hospital.

9. He will call you eventually. He will call you eventually. (Don't call him Girlfriend!) He will call you eventually. He will call you eventually. (Is it getting through?) He will call you eventually. (No, you shouldn't just call!) He will call you eventually. (No really, don't call him, whatever you do.) He will call you eventually, Girlfriend!

10. If you still want to call him, go back and read this section again and again until you regain your senses!

And another thing…

Girlfriend, don't get confused between not being a control freak and being too passive, lazy or selfish. While two sides of the same coin, these issues are equal in importance to avoid, but totally different. Being a control freak is exhibiting aggressive behavior to try to advance the relationship beyond a point that your guy has clearly exhibited he wants to go. Reciprocating and showing appreciation is "returning the favor" to a guy who you're confident is interested and who you're fairly certain is on the same page and at the same pace you are. Returning the favor is akin to returning a phone call. If he calls, call him back. If he doesn't call, don't call him. Give him the chance to call you on his own time. Returning the phone call is reciprocation; calling him because he hasn't called you when you want to talk, that's being a control freak!

MIY Maybe you think you don't need a man.

We live in fantastic times indeed. As I said before Girlfriend, you and your fantabulous self can be, do and have anything in this world you want. There's nothing stopping you. However, if you think that means you don't "need" a man, that mindset may be keeping you single.

It is absolutely true that you do not need a man for your basic survival. What an upgrade, Girlfriend, from the caveman days! We don't need a man to provide a home, food, financial stability or our fabulous set of handbags. We can do that all ourselves. So, the question arises, well then, what *do* you need him for? Life is not all about survival. Not anymore. Life is about the quest for personal fulfillment and self-development, not the accumulation of physical goods and material possessions. Life is about building connections, letting people challenge you and you challenging them – all without breaking the ties that bind.

Girlfriend, if you classify yourself as single, you do need a man. Besides the obvious baby-making role, you need a man to become un-single. You need a man to hold you at night. You need a man to be the person to grab your hand walking down the street. You need a man to take you to dinner. You need a man to look at you with the eyes that make you feel like the prettiest woman in the room. Sure, you will not *die* if you don't have a man. But will you really be living if you don't? That's the question you should be asking for yourself. Avoid the race to the bottom. This journey that is your life should not be about just getting by; it is about maximizing your personal growth and by extension, your happiness. The truth is, being in a real committed relationship is the gateway to some of life's lessons that you cannot get any other way. You just can't. There's no Cliff's Notes for this. You've just got to experience it. So, don't give yourself the b-s out from really putting the necessary work into yourself to make your relationships successful. Whatever is holding you back, let's tackle it, but Girlfriend please don't cop out and say "I don't need a man" because I think we can admit (at least between us girls) that for some pretty important things, you really do.

Still breathing my independent Girlfriend? Ok good. You're in control here, and that's the beautiful thing. You have the power to realize even though you can fully take care of yourself, you do have needs that aren't covered. They are not your survival needs, they are your personal fulfillment needs. And Girlfriend, your personal fulfillment is just as much your entitlement.

It's ok to have some vulnerability. We've all been through our fair share of man drama. Yes, I too have wanted to throw my hands up in the air and walk away, high-fiving my girlfriends down the path to permanent singledom, saying "I don't need a man, I can take care of myself" the entire length. But that path is a lonely one Girlfriend! And you're far too fabulous to be lonely. Give yourself permission to admit you have a weak spot, because you do. We all do. No matter your sexual preference, we all want someone to share our lives with, if not simply to satisfy that yearning for growth and intimacy that only certain levels of human interaction will provide. It's ok. It really is. It doesn't make you any less strong or less of a woman. In fact, it makes you the strongest type of woman. The woman who can and does acknowledge all of her needs of whatever nature and has the tools and courage to satisfy them.

MIY Maybe you haven't redefined gender roles.

One thing we all know is that the days of *Leave It to Beaver* are over by a long shot. Women are no longer just the keepers of the home. As the playing field equalizes on a personal and professional level, those convenient and simple "gender role" definitions have been all but obliterated. Nonetheless, that does not mean roles for each gender have now ceased to exist. Unfortunately, since nothing is settled other than the old rules no longer apply, men and women can't count on automatically being on the same page about what those roles are. So, Girlfriend, this is something you're going to have to separately establish for each relationship you're in. You don't have the luxury of assumptions (thank goodness!) and since none of us are June Cleaver, we have to let our guy know who we actually are, what his expectations should be of us and what our expectations are of him. It's a conversation that we now have to integrate into the fabric of the dating process.

I remember being confronted with this exact issue once with a man that I wanted to date, but couldn't understand why he wasn't pursuing me. We met at a Duke Alumni fundraiser. After a pretty interesting conversation, which eventually switched to golf, we decided it would be good to meet up some time on the links. Now, Girlfriend, I do not even pretend to be a good golf player, because I'm not at all. For me it was always just something I did to try to connect with my Dad who loves to play. So, I know my way around some clubs and a golf course, but in all honesty, I'm most at home at the driving range! So, Duke Alum and I decided to go to the driving range (so I wouldn't embarrass either of us) on a Sunday afternoon. We grabbed food afterwards and I went along my way. I had no idea whether or not it was a date and couldn't tell if he liked me. If you're curious (I know you are), he paid for dinner, but it could have just been a courteous friendly gesture for a number of reasons other than him considering it a romantic rendezvous. From there, he didn't really try to contact me that much; I think we had a couple of phone calls and emails exchanged, but nothing significant.

Eventually, we did decide to meet again for dinner. So, Girlfriend, if you don't know me by now, I'll tell you, of course I asked him directly what I found perplexing. Abruptly, in the middle of dinner I said, "So, Duke Alum, why haven't you asked me out? Are you dating someone? What's the deal?" He almost seemed relieved. And what he ultimately told me changed my perspective of modern dating forever. He said, "Well, women have always been my competition, in school and in the professional environment. So when I meet a woman, I really never know where she's coming from. I don't want to be wasting my time courting her for no reason and all the while she's just contributing to her 401K. I'd rather it be more of an equal landscape. If she lets me know up front what the deal is, then I can gauge how to proceed. Otherwise, I'm just casual about it and consider it meeting as friends until I'm certain it's otherwise."

Girlfriend, that was eye opening! I thought about it and I realized, this guy (and other guys too) must be scared out of their pants! Before, when they had the security of knowing that women weren't actually going to be real competition at work, they probably did feel a lot more comfortable spending money and paying for gifts and dates. However, if they're dating someone that is their professional competition, how would they know when to cross the line into a chivalrous space? I mean, just imagine if you're trying to date your counterpart at work and at the same time, you're competing against him for the one available promotion. You'd sleep with one eye open right? So one of the two of you would have to make it clear, given the circumstances, that despite the work competition, you were both romantically interested in one another and you'd have to figure the roles out from there! How complicated! But based on my research, that's how guys are viewing it. They don't know anymore if they're supposed to ask you out, pay for the date, open the door, whether you'll be offended or what you even expect. That's why an additional conversation has to be had. And Girlfriend, if you realize what's actually happening, this is great! This couldn't be more perfect! We all, you included, have the complete freedom for each guy we're with to define the role we want to play! That means, rather than him just assuming you're going to cook dinner, clean the house, do the laundry and watch the kids, you get to discuss and decide together what you're going to do and what he's going to do. *Vive la différence!*

With all this freedom, you don't have to be one thing or the other. You don't have to disavow your natural femininity or vulnerability just because you're making a successful way in what still is a man's world. Real freedom is the freedom to be you, whatever that is, and find success. It's the tension between like and not like that, in part, builds the attraction. A guy that's interested in women does not want to date himself. He wants "other than himself." So while you access your masculine energy, don't be afraid to also access whatever feminine energy that comes naturally to you. Thankfully the power is in your hands to define the dynamic. Let him open doors if that's what occurs to him. Sure, you can open your own doors, but it's up to you to help him define a "masculine" role in your life and determine together what that means. So, while you guys are figuring it out, don't take offense if he falls into the "traditional" role, for the time being. Just understand where it's coming from, accept it and make it part of the ongoing conversation. He's not doing anything wrong; he's just doing what he has been taught from whatever source is the right thing to do.

Girlfriend, this topic could be an entire book itself. The fact that gender roles are in flux is the best and worst thing to happen to dating in my lifetime. Traditional roles meant everyone was playing from the same playbook and could operate based on a set of fixed assumptions. Since that playbook has been virtually "blown up," you can't expect that a guy is going to act like what *you* think a prototypical "guy" should act like when you first meet him. Everybody's been playing by different rules. And all the girls he's dated before you probably each wanted something different! So, it's up to you Girlfriend to figure out what is going to work for you and feel it out with your guy. Find out what his prototype of the ideal woman is. Make the conversation light and fun. Ask him to pick the woman character from a television show that most corresponds to his ideal. That should tell you a lot. Then you can figure out not only what to expect from him initially, but also, what adjustments need to be made on both your parts to find a middle ground that works. But, if you assume that he's going to play some pre-determined role established in your mind, that presumption is going to keep you single and disappointed! Don't sell yourself short! Put in the work to first find out what you like and then communicate that to your guy. If he thinks you're worth it, he'll make the necessary adjustments. Also, and equally important, get to know what he likes. If you think he's worth it as well, you make your necessary adjustments. The upside here Girlfriend is that you can make the changes because you *want to* not because you have to.

MIY Maybe you live in New York City or Los Angeles.

I remember vividly when I had just moved to Los Angeles, at a Fourth of July party I attended with one of my girlfriends, I was thoroughly entertained by a very brazen, opinionated, hilarious and knowledgeable woman who went back and forth between spilling the beans with tales of Hollywood celebrity indiscretions and creative little statements about her own views on life. At the time I was 26, and she was 29, so I looked at her as a fountain of mature wisdom. The one thing she said that stood out in my mind was her pronouncement that she was imminently moving to Texas. I thought to myself, "Wait a minute! What is this super-cool, clearly fast-lane, career-track having, fun and exciting woman doing moving to Texas? Are you serious?" But, Girlfriend, the shock of all shocks was her reasoning. When asked why, without hesitation or shame of any sort, she said easily, "Because I want to get married! I will not be single and 30 in LA!" At the time, I thought, wow, either she's crazy or she knows something I don't. Girlfriend, I've crossed the 5 year mark in LA and I can tell you with almost certainty that she was anything but crazy.

If you don't live in Los Angeles or New York City, it's still worthwhile to visit this section. For one, you'll get a glimpse into what the "big city" girlfriends are dealing with, and you'll think twice if you're deciding to move and you have other options… well, of course, unless you like being single.

Let me start off by saying that LA and NYC are magnificent cities to live in. They have bright lights, beautiful people, and endless possibilities of things to do. Love it or not Girlfriend, but it is exactly the plethora of distractions that are keeping you single. While you derive rapturous pleasure from living in the city because it allows you to focus on your career, find things to do when you're not working, and meet an endless supply of new people, just remember that guys in town have the exact same options. Dating in LA and NYC is like going fishing in a whirlpool. These are meeting and casual dating cities. I've lived in both and I can tell you it's true. NYC, people go to make their fortune. That's their number one objective. LA is not much different. People come to LA to see what or who they can become. These people are going for the real gusto in life – the high risk, high reward true "gamblers." That means for their efforts, they likely want a "trophy" for a girlfriend, and the decision to make her a wife will not be easy because the alternatives are so plentiful. Girlfriend, LA is like the NBA of attractive women – a city where people of all sorts get by just on their physical appearance, or at least are led to believe they can. That's why gorgeous people are around every corner. They all come to LA to see how far their looks (and marginally, their talent) can take them. If you're in that mix, good luck!

New York is a city where cash is king. I remember that dating an investment banker in NYC one summer was literally the worst dating experience of my life. So bad in fact, I used to call him "Terrible G" – to his face.

The culture of his business taught him that as long as he was making money, nothing else mattered. All behaviors will be excused. That was Terrible G's license to treat me like a possession. Not a prized possession mind you, but just like some bauble he picked up at the store. Where LA is about looks, NYC is about the resume, and the package. Yes, I totally am generalizing, Girlfriend, but I'd rather tell you the rule and let you hope to be the exception on your own. I'm not saying you shouldn't live in NYC or LA, but I am saying that these are both cities where people are focused on other things besides marriage and tend to wait until later to make permanent couplings if at all.

I single out NYC and LA, because these are the two fastest-paced cities with the most distractions, both work and cultural. Distractions serve their intended purpose. They keep you and your guy distracted from each other and the relationship. If you live in an area with fewer distractions, you have fewer reasons not to look to each other for the stimulation you crave. If dating is all that's available to do on the weekends, then that's what will happen. Trust me, as a good old girl from the Midwest, I know those harsh winters were always the absolute BEST time to get a guy. Everyone, men and women, wanted to avoid going out as much as possible, so what did we all do? Get someone quickly to spend those evenings with you in your warm house!

If you live in LA or NYC, don't panic. I'm not telling you to move. At least, I'm not saying you have to move not to be single. But, what I am saying is be aware of the social identity of where you are geographically. Why do you live in those cities? Most likely you did not move there to improve your dating options. You moved for work, play or otherwise. So did your prospective guy! Dating is not the first thing on anyone's list! So what to do, right Girlfriend?

Well, at least now that you know what you're working with, you've got to be creative in how you're meeting and dating. Instead of looking in bars, clubs and lounges, try cultural events, sporting (*e.g.*, the gym or the golf course), and professional organizations. I would even say a work romance shouldn't be out of the question. Also, we'll discuss this later, but, more than anywhere else, you should be registered with the online dating service of your choice. For a very large percentage of the recent marriages of people I know in LA and NY, the couple met online. It's $30 a month, Girlfriend! You might meet a few guys from the "defective" bin, but that's ok, throw them back and keep at it until you meet someone that works for you. As for me, roughly 75% of my LA dating initiates from Match.com. The other non-traditional places I meet great guys are: (1) fundraisers, (2) entertainment industry invite-only events (*e.g.*, screenings, launch parties, wrap parties, etc.), (3) salsa clubs (4) classes (*e.g.*, comedy, acting, fitness, etc.), and (funny enough) (5) airplanes/the airport. When I lived in NY, I was younger, so the majority of places that I met men were either at work or at lounges and clubs. If you're a NY Girlfriend and you're looking for alternatives, I would suggest summer concerts, the gym, alumni events and fundraisers.

Bottom line, just understanding the dating culture of where you live is a huge head start on making some real romance happen there! You don't necessarily have to move like many girlfriends have, but if you stay, you will likely have to be open to getting a later start on more permanent relationships and possibly long-distance dating. Just don't let those bright lights in the big city keep you single!

MIY Maybe you don't set and stick to standards.

Your Standards are the soldiers that keep you safe from the losers running around posing as datable guys. Why would you sacrifice them unnecessarily? Standards go to battle for you in every relationship – that is, if you let them. So many of the girlfriends, thinking that they have met the next unrestored Picasso of a man accept a less than stellar guy into their lives and run with it until literally every member of the proverbial band stops playing. Girlfriend! You set your floor and never go beneath it!

Once you start compromising your Standards, you start becoming susceptible to those dangerous enemies of happiness: desperation, delusion and disappointment. How do you know when you're unacceptably compromising your established floor? Good question. First, by defining what you want. After you define what you want, set your dealbreakers. Only you know what works for you. Don't get caught up in politically-correct guidelines for what you should or shouldn't do. The only thing you shouldn't do when dating is compromise your Standards.

Many of the girlfriends will actually opt to date a guy's "Ifhethen" rather than just accepting the reality that they are with someone who doesn't make the grade. **If he**

__________, and the blank could be filled with absolutely anything, got a job, lost some weight, had more hair, wasn't married, wasn't a cheater, etc.; **then** the relationship would be "so much better." Ugh! Girlfriend, at what point do we realize the he is *never* going to change? That guy is *never* going to see the other side of that "if." He is who he is and unless it becomes a problem for "him" directly, then it's *your* problem, and only your problem. You are not dating his Ifhethen. You're just dating plain old him and that's all it's ever going to be. Ifhethen only exists in your mind.

Girlfriend, my experience with dropping my standards certainly left me extremely unhappy and *single* on a number of occasions. Most recently, I dropped my Standard that the guy I'm with be fit and live a physically active and healthy lifestyle, to date a guy that was significantly overweight and extremely sedentary. Of course, in thinking that he could be "the One," I set about enjoying his company and the activities and interests that we shared, which involved mainly eating, rather than going to the gym, hiking or other active pastimes. In the three months that we dated, while I was thinking everything would be perfect *if* he just started taking his health seriously, he was gaining weight… and so was I, Girlfriend. I gained fifteen pounds! When we broke up, sweating myself back into my regular jeans, I realized why I had set the healthy living Standard and why I should have never dropped it in the first place.

The beautiful thing about Standards is that no matter where the relationship leads, they ensure that you are going to feel ok. You don't have to explain them to anybody and in all of your fabulousness, they are your entitlement.

Every performing musician has what is called a "rider" which is added to each performance agreement for their appearances. The artist rider lists in specificity the accommodations that the artist needs in order to perform and is supposed to represent the minimum requirements for an artist's comfort. It is not intended to create their home away from home. A rider that is too outlandish has led to the cancellation of many an engagement to perform, even for some of the most in-demand acts. Their needs were just impossible to meet! I've heard that some of the biggest divas want all-white rooms filled with roses and the temperature set at exactly 72 degrees before they enter. Girlfriend, that is out of control! So with this in mind, what is on your rider? What do you need before you "show up" for a relationship and bestow a guy with all of your wonderful womanly delights? Do not sell yourself short; but on the other hand, don't set yourself up for a "cancelled engagement" either!

A WORD ABOUT *Standards vs. other objective criteria...*

Girlfriend, in this book, I'm going to say two things repeatedly. One, don't abandon your Standards, and two, move away from using only objective criteria to evaluate prospective guys. Seemingly contradictory right? In a way, yes. Standards are objective criteria. However, the important distinction here is that Standards should establish your baseline from a perspective of what will and will not work for you in a relationship. Standards protect you from the negative effects of characteristics that based on your personal experience or good old common sense, result in a negative experience for you. Objective criteria, if too specific and based on irrational wants, rather than needs, only serve to limit your dating options. An example of a Standard is that a man be employed. An example of objective criteria is that the man be a doctor or a lawyer, an athlete or magician – that's not a Standard, that's an unnecessary limitation that will keep you single!

MIY Maybe you're selfish.

Most of the girlfriends are going to read this and immediately say, "No way is this me!" And I say to you Girlfriend, hold on one second. Behaviors and thoughts that you don't think are selfish most likely are, and even worse, they're keeping you single. Being selfish goes beyond simply putting yourself first. It involves putting yourself at the center of the universe and expecting all things and all people to revolve around you. From your place of importance, you make judgments and interpretations based on your own frame of reference. You assume that everyone thinks like you do, would react as you would react, would like what you like and you reach your conclusions accordingly. Let's say you like flowers and your guy hates to use the phone (as most guys do). Your guy calls you everyday, but you're extra-super upset that he hasn't sent you flowers yet. Meanwhile, you make no acknowledgement of his efforts to call you on a regular basis. Is that being selfish? Yes, Girlfriend, it is. It is a failure to interpret your guy's actions based on what they mean to him, rather than to you and you only. Sometimes you have to step out of your own shoes and look at the world through another person's eyes to understand the full picture. Many times when you think your guy doesn't care or isn't making a special effort for you, he actually is, but you're not in a position to recognize it. Let's face it, women and men do not speak the same language, want the same things, share the same motivations or enjoy themselves the same way. So, continuing the above example, if your guy hates talking on the phone, understand what that means when he calls you.

If your guy is doing something you like, the next step is to take notice of what he likes and meet him on his level. Is he taking you out to dinner all the time? Then by the fourth or fifth date, you need to reciprocate in some way. Offer a meal, or a concert or tickets to a sporting event. Whatever you choose, the decision should be about him and what he would like to do, rather than what you want to do or think that he would want to do. Put in the work and ask your male friends, ask your dad, your cousins or even a cabbie, but don't make an assumption and get it wrong. That's selfish and selfish girlfriends are single.

Try to find a common ground with your guy without compromising your core needs or your Standards. The first step is to stop assuming that everything he does or says means what it would if you did or said it (or didn't do or say it). Taking that one step would make a world of difference in your breaking away from selfish tendencies. It allows you to shift the center of your universe from you to someone else when the time comes to reach a conclusion about another's actions. Each guy you meet is operating in the world with his own set of experiences and preferences. Believe it or not, Girlfriend, it is not all about you.

If you want some practice shifting focus, start by volunteering. Taking action for the pure benefit of another gets your mind into the framework needed to open yourself up to including a guy in your life. Relationships take work, compromise and some sacrifice. Girlfriend, the only circumstance that alllows you to have it all your way all the time is when you're paying for it... or, when you're single.

MIY Maybe you don't think you're fabulous.

Girlfriend, make no mistake, you ARE fabulous! You are a unique, wonderful, intelligent, talented, fantastic creature who deserves the absolute best that this world has to offer her! I'm sure I am not the only person with that opinion and I hope the president of your fan club is YOU! If not,

Girlfriend, you've got a serious problem on your hands. The first person to think that you're wonderful has to be you. You're great because of all the lessons you've learned, mistakes you've made, challenges you've overcome and many other experiences that are the particular way you came to be the person you are. If you think you are undeniably fabulous, chances are other people will as well. In fact, a little self-esteem goes a long way. But, on the other hand, a woman missing her self-esteem is like a designer car missing its engine. If you don't think you're fabulous, people will know! Then, you become discounted goods at the dating supermarket. If you don't know your value, you'll accept less than your worth and then you wind up with some loser that I only hope for your sake disappears quickly.

Many of the girlfriends are in denial about their fabulosity because in dating, you tend to judge yourself based on superficial qualities that you believe men are interested in. That means, you're focused on your beauty, your weight, whether or not your thighs look fat, all the things that ultimately don't matter. Actually, to be honest, Girlfriend, they do matter, but not as much as you think they do. The reality is, if you're pitting yourself against all of the other women in your city in a beauty competition, you'd lose. There is always going to be another prettier face. If you're trying to be the thinnest, if you survive the eating disorder, you'd lose again. There's always going to be someone thinner. So as you start down this path of horribles, and it makes you feel worse and worse, you should be beginning to see there's no way to win on objective criteria alone. You have no real control over your superficial qualities. If as a looker you're a 7, you're a 7. So what you'll never be a 10. You don't need to be! That's why I say forget this line of thinking! Think of your set of oldest and closest friends. Are you concerned whether or not they like you? Hopefully not, Girlfriend! Why is that? Isn't it because you realize your friends like you based on a whole host of intangible characteristics that make you the person you are? When it's a friend, you're completely secure because you'd never think that they're focused on your superficial qualities. You presume they like you for your unique and positive traits that you are not insecure about (your humor, intelligence, thoughtfulness, etc.). That's for good reason. They're yours alone, so the field of competition is narrowed to one, you! So, as you start to think of yourself in a dating capacity, don't head down the road of wondering does he think you're pretty enough, or smart enough or tall enough or any of the other characteristics that make you feel less than confident and fabulous. Focus on those qualities that you're sure about. If you have a difficult time identifying them, think of why your friends like you. The more energy you spend on emphasizing the qualities you're sure about, the more they will shine through and the more unique and intriguing you become.

Most of all, don't try to be perfect. Fabulous is not perfect. Fabulous is the crazy, silly, bad humor-having, clumsy, wonderful woman who wears braces and pointy-rimmed glasses – as long as she thinks herself to be fabulous.

Girlfriend, find your fabulous! Right now! Make yourself a list of 10 positive attributes that you have and one kicker. The kicker is one thing you can name about yourself that you have or can do better than anyone else you know. Your kicker may be as simple as "I can hula-hoop longer than all of my girlfriends." Then if that's the case, expand on that one thing. Start doing what you're good at and emphasizing what you have going for you. Live within that list of 11 qualities and begin to work on yourself. Then, answer this question: I would be so much better if I ___________. Whether you fill that blank with "lost 10 pounds," "changed my hair color," "went back to school," or even "got a new job," do it and love yourself in the process, even if it's just for becoming closer to the woman you want to be!

If You're Not Meeting Anyone, Maybe It's You...

MIY Maybe you're fat.

The harshest and most emotional criticism that I hear many of my girlfriends levy against themselves time and time again is "I'm so fat." They stand in the mirror for a collective period of hours and hours squeezing, pulling and inspecting - grabbing pinches of fat, sometimes only a fold of skin really and then they spit out with disgust, "Look at this! I'm so gross!" Really? Most of the time, all I can think to myself is, are you freakin' serious? In no world is a size 6 fat. Not at any height or at any weight. Ironically, it's the skinny girls who are obsessed with thinking that they're fat and it's the truly pudgy girls who couldn't care less. If you ask one of the latter, she would probably casually say, "Well, to think about it, yeah, I could probably stand to lose a few pounds," but she's too busy to really spend time talking about it because she is headed off on a date with her boyfriend. And you, my "fat" single Girlfriend, what are you up to? With all this time to yourself, you're likely obsessing.

Is your fat keeping you single? No, mostly likely not. What's keeping you single is your perception of yourself. I remember a guy I recently dated while at my heaviest, about 30 pounds fluffier than usual. To make myself feel more confident on our first date, I splurged a little on a flattering outfit and spent extra time on my hair and makeup. I might have been fluffy, but on that date, I truly did feel fabulous! I spent that evening sitting across from this fit, attractive, successful man who told me repeatedly throughout our well-planned and lovely evening how attractive I looked. And then later, as we sat finishing our dessert, he spoke about his previous relationship that he ended because his girlfriend had gained weight. How much weight? 20 pounds. I thought about that on our second date, and our third date, but by our fourth, I figured whatever it was, *my* weight must not matter to him. Go figure. Lesson learned? It doesn't always boil down to your fat cells, Girlfriend. What is even more obvious than the often-times non-existent fat roll you're grabbing is your absence of self-esteem and confidence. If you think you're disgusting or gross, what do you expect the guy to think? It reads all over you. You don't accentuate what you do have in the way you dress, you don't stand up straight, and you don't scream with your movements and actions, "Look at me, I'm a sexy goddess!" What you think you are is reflected to others you encounter, men especially. Just like animals read fear, men read weak-willed women and they dismiss them immediately.

Lest anyone be confused, this is not to say that you should commence an unhealthy lifestyle. That, Girlfriend, will keep you single. The most important element to your appearance is that you look healthy! Healthy means a lower waist to hip ratio, clear skin, clear eyes, shiny hair, and a general glow of vitality. So, before you order the extra serving of french fries, let me clarify. Bottom line, you need to love yourself.

The unfortunate thing about thinking you're fat is if you can't be convinced otherwise, even if you are not *really* fat, it will still come across to the people you meet. So, Girlfriend, if you truly believe in your heart of hearts that you have 20 pounds to lose before anyone will want you, then unless it will leave you at a seriously unhealthy weight, most likely, you're going to have to go ahead and lose those 20 pounds. Assuming you choose a healthy path, hopefully the process of exercise will make you start to feel better generally, and, most importantly, better about your self image.

If you really are tipping the scales a bit, it is hard to be self-confident. But the women that are, world watch out! What you should be concerned with beyond aesthetics is living healthy and smart. You should be making wise choices for your body and mind to make sure that you're around to enjoy the guy you ultimately do meet as long and as much as possible.

If you really think you're fat, the danger here is that you're not in the greatest position to let your internal beauty fly. If there's something you want to change about yourself, especially if it's your weight, and it's the healthy thing to do, by all means stop complaining and get to changing it! But in the meantime, find some things about yourself that you really do like and *emphasize* them! I know for me, the blessing to the curse of weight gain is some extra filling up top. I may have to take my jeans up a size, but can I be mad if my bra cup size goes up too? I'll tell you this, it did not hurt me at all with the men folk.

MIY Maybe you don't work out.

Since this is not about being fat or thin and purely about being healthy, unless you've been blessed with the super-gene, you need to be active. This is about you breaking a sweat on a regular basis. Why? Let's talk for a minute about the benefits of exercise. Not only does it get your valuable heart muscle working, but these lovely chemicals called endorphins are released in the process. These fabulous little bundles of pure joy hit the happy centers in your brain and make you a gleaming ray of "look at me, I'm fabulous!" light. The circulation also hits your cheeks and helps to add a natural "rosy" glow to your already beautiful face. Not to mention, those problem areas that like to spread and threaten your expulsion from your too-expensive designer jeans, get controlled and minimized. And one more thing… guess where men like to congregate? In the gym! Why would you pass on this amazing all-in-one opportunity!

Now, let me get extra-real for a second. Most men, especially those that take their health and fitness level seriously, do not want an unhealthy woman. Many would take it so far as to say they don't want to date someone who is overweight. Before you panic, what a man actually considers "overweight" varies from man to man, and is different for each woman. In Los Angeles, "overweight" means something totally different than what it does in Atlanta. Girlfriend, I'm not trying to give you a complex, but I am trying to keep it 100% honest for you. So I'm going to say something that most of your girlfriends will not tell you: if you are overweight, and I mean at an unhealthy weight (not 10 pounds, but 30 + pounds), as you're probably suspecting deep down yourself, it could very much be keeping you single.

Here's the reality, and this is coming from someone who has had a lifelong struggle with managing her own weight, yes, men should like you for you; however, that does not necessarily translate into wanting to have sex with you. You know the saying "men are from Mars, women are from Venus?" Well for the purpose of this conversation, I'd like to change that to "men like to look, and they think with their penis." Translated, that means men are visual creatures. They "think" based on what their eyes see at the moment and they do not operate on potential. They do not look at you in a bar, see your fat rolls hanging out over your jeans and think, "Oh, she must be on a diet, that's all gonna change soon, so I'll just decide that I want to sleep with her now anyway." What actually happens is they just don't see what they're looking for and they keep it moving. Women are the ones that are more adept at looking past what they see and letting their thoughts of the person shape their physical experience.

For men, there is a distinct difference between your value to him as a person, and his physical attraction to you. Try as you might to be the coolest woman in the world, you can talk sports, shoot pool and drink with the best of them, but if you do not look "healthy" to him, then you'll land in the "friend zone," faster than a fly ball gets called by the umpire. I'm not telling you that you need to be stick thin to find a guy. That is 100% untrue. But you do need to look "healthy" to him for him to find you attractive. Physical attraction for men is a fully-separate issue. They are unable to be physically intimate with someone they are not attracted to (like we are). It's just a biological reality. It is not personal and it is not wrong. It is not mean or intentionally hurtful. That's just how it is. The good news is you can do something about it. While you do not want to be obsessive and call yourself "fat" when you're not, especially because it is annoying and wastes time and energy no one has to spare, you do need to be honest with yourself about when you can shed some extra mass that is truly affecting your self-esteem and the way men view you. There is nothing wrong with hitting the gym a few times a week.

And when you do hook that guy, you're going to want some things to do where you can "connect" on a physical basis without having to rely on sex. Men like physical exertion and the intensity around it. If they like you, they would love nothing more than to combine it all! So why not go on a hike, or roller-blading, running, walking, dancing, playing some basketball or take it old-school and get to the roller-skating rink. You won't regret it and feel free to thank me later!

If you're wondering whether or not guys think you're healthy, first start with you. Ask yourself if you are actually living a healthy lifestyle. Are you paying attention to what you're eating and making wise food choices in terms of types of food and quantity? Do you work out at least 3 times per week? If you're really honest with yourself, you know the answer. Still, for real verification, ask your best guy friend to be completely honest with you with no negative recourse. He's likely going to say something in an attempt not to hurt your feelings, but in this conversation, Girlfriend, you want honesty! So, do your best to reassure him that he can tell you the truth and make sure that you prepare yourself for whatever he says. For an objective, professional opinion, ask your physician or talk to a trainer at a local gym.

And speaking of the gym, get to one! If you don't want to make the financial commitment, sign up for a trial membership and sample the classes. Make it fun. You just might like it and be willing to take the leap. At minimum, buy or borrow an exercise video to use at home. Don't want to be indoors? Head outside (if it's not cold, harsh winter, of course) and take a 30-50 minute walk. If you like how that feels (how could you not, my lazy Girlfriend), ramp the time up and then, up the intensity. Whatever you do, just get moving!

MIY Maybe you're overly pessimistic.

Girlfriend, has so much gone wrong in your dating past that you're now "over it" and pretty much think what can go wrong will go wrong? If so, those types of thoughts are most certainly keeping you single. Beyond the typical "men are dogs" conversation, many of the girlfriends happily (or unhappily) skip down the road of negativity much like Dorothy in the *Wizard of Oz*. Except Girlfriend, this road isn't bright yellow and filled with companions of the male variety. This road is dusty, difficult, dark and generally depressing. What you think defines your perspective and your perspective is how you experience reality. The "is the glass half full or half empty" question is real! If you see the glass as half empty and you are only viewing things from the negative, nothing could possibly go right, unless it was absolutely perfect. That's a lot of enjoyment you're missing.

We have all been through some absolute rotten bananas in the world of dating, and even slipped on the peel after the fact, but consider this not par for the course, but exactly what the learning process is. With dating, I realize that it's really important and you just want it to go well *so badly*. Everyone wants and deserves to be loved, Girlfriend. But we all have to learn how to love and be loved. We need to give ourselves the latitude to make bad choices before we come to a conclusion right? In school, if you failed your first three math tests for the semester, did you quit? Not unless you dropped out, Girlfriend! You had to figure out a way to make it work to graduate. The same goes for dating and relationships. You can throw your hands up and say "I just can't figure this out" and keep your negative attitude, but that just makes you a dating drop out! Do what you did in school, get a tutor and start figuring out how to solve those difficult problems!

If you expect the worst, how can you recognize when you're getting something good? If Prince Charming himself approached a negative woman, she'd be skeptical all the way through from his shoes to his clothes to his princely demeanor. She'd question his motives behind every single action and constantly ask why instead of enjoying what, as in, what he's doing for her. She'd tell her other girlfriends, yeah he seems cool now, but I've been down this road before... Girlfriend! You have to let go of the past! Maybe you've kissed a few frogs. Ok, then learn to recognize frogs a bit earlier before you kiss them. Assumptions are for lazy people. Making assumptions takes the work out of having to analyze and interpret each person and situation you encounter on an individual basis. That takes time, work and thought. So, don't *assume* that every man you meet is going to be a frog!

Girlfriend to Girlfriend

SUGGESTION

Girlfriend, get your expectations out of the dumps! Seriously, all the crap that you've dealt with to this point is just that, crap! It does not mean all situations you deal with in the future are going to present the same experiences! Stop trying to protect yourself by expecting the worst. That's just cheating yourself. Worse, it's too harsh of a punishment for the bad decisions you've made in the past. Define this as what it really is – a mistake (or series of mistakes) that you should learn from and do better. Call them the exception rather than the rule - the trail of frogs until you meet your guy. Just remember though, if you're in the forest and something passes by, if it is little and green, it hops, it has little buggy eyes and bumpy skin, and most importantly if it **tells you it is a frog**, ok, it's probably a frog. But does that mean you should exit the forest immediately? No, Girlfriend! Identify the frog for what it is and look for something different. There are so many other types of guys out there than what you've encountered in your past. Don't turn a fox into a frog just because a frog is what you're used to. That's all I'm saying!

A WORD ABOUT *the scarcity of men...*

The most pessimistic thing that the girlfriends say repeatedly is, "There are no men!" No matter the context, in college, in a city or town, of a particular ethnic group, or even working at a company, this belief rings loudly from the highest rooftops as the misery chorus sings the refrain over and over again. Girlfriend, seriously, despite what everyone else may be saying, there is no shortage of men. If you listen to the reports and the constant whining, you would think that you could walk around the city for days and see not one single man. We all know that this is not truly the case. So before you get caught up in statistics like what percentage of men are in some way unavailable, leaving only X percent for you, let me say this: you are not dating a percentage. You are not dating the odds. You are dating a single individual. If only 30% of the male population is "datable," you do not need it to be 31% before you find your guy. All you need is one guy, *and specifically the* one guy *that is right for you. The doomsday interpretations of the statistics are just guessing games. You could find the person that best fits you in a population of 1% available men. What you* really *should be concerned about is* you *not being prepared, men-*

tally, spiritually, physically, emotionally and financially, when that right person comes along.

MIY Maybe you are unhappy.

Happy girlfriends get dates. Remember that. Almost every guy that I've asked why he chose the woman he's with listed "happy" in some way amongst the qualities named. Let's just be real about this my grumpy Girlfriend. Happy people are magnets for other people. The joy and positivity that a happy person emits even makes them look better. So if you're not glowing with your own little candle of contentment, then we totally have a problem.

Girlfriend, being unhappy with yourself, your job, your life, your home, your weight, or even your hair extensions is a state of affairs that makes you preoccupied with something other than being your best self, whatever that is at the time. The root of your unhappiness is not only a distracting focal point, but also a severe crack in your emotional foundation that most likely makes you needy and annoying in relationships. I know, I've been there. There was a period in my life during which I was severely unhappy about my job and my place. My place was too small and my job was too demanding. I wasn't making enough money to even meet my fixed expenses. In short, I was miserable! How, I don't know, but I was seeing a guy at the time who was fun and exciting. He had his own successful business, so not only did he make a comfortable amount of money, but he also had the luxury of determining his own schedule for each day. Unsurprisingly, I was all about this guy, spending all my time with him and really using him as a distraction from the things in my life that were making me sad.

What's the problem here? There were two. First, as fun and distracting as this guy was, he was a capital jerk on more than one occasion. He'd be unreliable and disrespectful when we were out. Second, he was unwilling to commit to a monogamous relationship, even after three months of dating. And what did I do, I stayed in the situation and dealt with the drama. Why? Because rather than solving the problems that I had in my life, I looked at him as my solution. I thought I "needed" him emotionally, figuring that he would "rescue" me from my woes eventually and I'd have nothing more to worry about. Ugh! One day, as he set about again pointing out my flaws and the flaws in my life, I realized I wasn't hiding anything. He easily identified the things that were making me unhappy and he viewed them as "drawbacks" to dating me. At that moment, I realized I needed someone in my life who was going to help me fix my flaws, rather than someone who was just going to sit there and point them out, and the first and best person for that was ME. So, I got rid of the guy, changed jobs, and rather than getting a new place, I just cleaned up the old one – threw out a lot of junk and had the carpet cleaned. Once I handled the issues that were bothering me and making me unhappy, my mental and emotional stability improved. That process allowed me to give the next guy more physical and emotional space and made me a lot less needy. Needy girlfriends are single!

Hey there Sunshine! If you're in the dumps, you're gonna get dumped. It's that simple. If you're unhappy and you're dating someone, you are probably exhibiting behavior best described as annoying and needy. Think of a guy you've dated in the past that you would characterize using the same terms. Seriously, Girlfriend, that's exactly how you're making your guy feel about you! Wanting to be around him all of the time is puppy love. Having to be around him all the time makes you a cling-on. That's not cute, my little Raincloud, not cute at all. Instead of making him your human Prozac, you need to take the time to identify the things that specifically are making you unhappy. Parse them out one at a time. Once you have your list, dedicate time away from dating to tackle solving those problems. If those problems don't have a readily visible solution, don't give up. If necessary, get advice from other people (including possibly a therapist). If you're really, really unhappy, dating is not going to work. So rather than turn off a potentially good guy because you weren't fully baked, take a break and focus on you. It's not time wasted Girlfriend, it's a disaster averted!

MIY Maybe you get wrapped up in the ideal of what you're supposed to want.

Our Standards start pretty high, don't they Girlfriend? First when we're little girls, we're told that we are "princesses" and in every story we hear about a princess, she winds up with a prince, no matter if she has been asleep for 1000 years or locked away in a heavily guarded tower. And, of course, we never quite realize that this is just a so-called "fairy-tale." How cruel is it to tell me something for the first 10-12 years of my life and then switch it at the last minute? I mean, Santa Claus was trauma enough. Don't take away my prince too! But then, Girlfriend, we trade the Cinderella fantasy for the "Career-erella" one. We become the modern-day working "princess" and we set out looking for our modern-day prince. Oh and what a package that prince would be, tall (but not too tall), devastatingly handsome (but still rugged), an athlete's build (but not too muscular), intelligent (but not nerdy), poised (but not stuck-up), humble (yet confident), wealthy (but generous), funny (but not goofy). And it wouldn't hurt if he was a surgeon to boot, right? Oh, Girlfriend. Break free of the chains! If you want to see what real princesses wind up with, catch a couple of episodes of "Platinum Weddings." As lovely as the weddings are and as beautiful as the stories are of the romance that led up to the big day, those guys are anything but the true life replica of Prince Charming. They are not perfect and, in fact, they are flawed. They might not be as devastatingly handsome, they might be balding or bald, and they might be a little more goofy than funny. But if you saw how they treated their brides, your heart would melt immediately and you'd "get it" right away. These flawed men profess their loved to their flawed women in a way that could bring a tear to your eye (I'll admit it, I've cried!!). People are not perfect, Girlfriend, but relationships can be.

Don't get so wrapped up in the ideal of what you're supposed to want that you miss out on what will ultimately make you happy. You're not dating as part of a competition with your girlfriends! Your mothers are not sitting on a judging panel holding up scores at lunch time: "Yeah, Jodi's guy is tall, smart and successful, but where's his summer home? I only give him an 8." It doesn't happen like that! And even if it did, why do you care what your mother's friends think?

And remember, even though our beloved *Sex and the City's* Carrie wound up with Mr. Big, this was only after he treated her like a bauble that didn't matter, married another woman in the middle of their relationship, made her his mistress while he cheated on his wife, and jilted her at their own wedding. And let's not forget that he watched, frozen in time, while his supposed beloved had a mental breakdown in the middle of a busy Manhattan street! After she tapes together the pieces of her broken heart, she can look forward to sleeping with one eye open the rest of their lives together.

Girlfriend, don't get blinded by the ideal of your own "Mr. Big." Looking for him is going to keep you single. Focus on what really matters, and you might just be surprised.

Don't get caught up in the confusion of what you're supposed to want. Like Santa Claus and Unicorns, you should have figured out by now that the "perfect guy" doesn't exist. All you get is the guy that is perfect for you. And I can guarantee that he'll be pretty amazing. For you to cut past all the crap and get to what really matters, you're going to need to move off of objective criteria (*e.g.*, height, income, appearance), and, keeping in mind your Standards, move to the subjectives that we first talked about in "Maybe you don't know what you want" (e.g., he makes me *feel* _______). So instead of waiting for the guy you think that everyone else will label a prince, go get *your* guy. Sure, you're going to kiss a few frogs along the way, and yes, they'll actually be frogs, but if you're diligent, one might just turn into the man that makes you feel like a real princess!

MIY Maybe you're not interacting with enough people.

Girlfriend, let's imagine you received a beautiful pair of expensive antique earrings as a gift. They were amazing when you got them, but needed a replacement for one of the missing stones, so you had them repaired, perfected, cleaned and polished. Once the earrings were shiny, beautiful and fabulous, you put them into a jewelry box and stuffed them in your drawer. Wait. You'd never do that would you? Absolutely not! You and I both know the next logical step with those earrings is to wear them out, even if it's just to the grocery store. Why hide all that hard-perfected beauty right? The same goes with you, Girlfriend! After all the work you put into making yourself phenomenal, why are you hiding? Single women are meant to be seen and heard!

Dating is a numbers game and the only way to start playing is to meet people. That means you have to be accessible. Easy to find, not that easy to get. That's our motto here. To be accessible, you have to be out and interacting with people. You've got to be living in the world and put yourself in a position to collide with Mr. Right, or Mr. Right-Now, whatever the case may be! And you have to put yourself out there shamelessly. Shame is for wimps!

Several of the girlfriends that I've talked to about this have said they think any real attempt to put themselves out there

makes them appear "desperate" to find someone. Well, let me ease your concerns here. You are not trying to find someone, you are helping someone find you. Additionally, desperation is when you start dropping your Standards that make sense (not the crazy rules and requirements that you made up), in the effort to compromise your way to being in a relationship. Desperation is not making a reasonable compromise, but rather evidenced by you compromising yourself and your core values. Taking yourself from a 7 to a 6, just because you want a man in your life. Actively putting yourself out there to meet someone is not doing that.

First thing I'm going to say, in this day and age, if you're single and you're not a member of at least one online dating site, you're being ridiculous. So what if you don't want people to know you're out there looking. Guess what Girlfriend, they already know! If you look down at your left hand ring finger and there's no ring, everyone that sees you can guess with reasonable certainty that you're single! It's not a secret! You should hope that "they" know you're actively looking to meet someone; they might know someone for you. And, if "they" see you on an online dating service, then that means "they" were browsing there too! Hello! There's no online dating police that carefully review profiles and then generate a report for all your friends and family. It's just your own fear of trying something new that's getting in the way.

A WORD ABOUT *online dating...*

Girlfriend, I'm not going to tell you specifically which service to try. Ideally, you'll try all of them. There are plenty of books that give you helpful hints on setting up your profile and other strategies to maximize that dating avenue.

One piece of advice that I do have from my own experience is you really should approach all people you meet online from the perspective of being friends first. Just because you click with someone initially, do not even pretend to head down the romantic path until you see each other in person. It's tempting to do so. The emails are good; he's writing witty things that make you laugh... you find yourself looking forward to the next message. Then, you start talking on the phone... and he's got a good phone voice and all is well... until *you meet in person. Remember Girlfriend when I said that often the difference between a platonic friendship and a romantic relationship is physical attraction? That's where this comes into play. When you meet online, you don't get an opportunity to gauge your physical attraction to each other at first. However, given the nature of how you met – online* dating, *the automatic presumption is you're meeting for the purpose of entering into a romantic relationship. Only, without a sense of the physical connection, you have no idea whether or not that essential chemistry is going to be there. So, the best thing to do is to pump the brakes and stress the friendship. Setting up friendship as the expectation leaves you both open to get to know each other better and you don't have to make an immediate decision based on first impressions when you finally do meet. It could be that you are only meant to be friends (like if you show up and he looks like the crypt keeper, but perfectly nice guy though), or the friendship you are establishing could grow into something more if you give it the time and opportunity to develop. Just because it is "online* dating," *doesn't mean everyone you meet will be someone you're going to date. Instead of using it as an automatic entrée into a relationship, look at it more as a way to meet more friends - friends to go to coffee with, friends to have dinner with, and friends to introduce you to their friends. Your online peeps don't have to necessarily turn into "boyfriends."*

Girlfriend, get out there and try some new things, especially new activities. They could be your key to meeting someone. For example, one of my mother's best friends is always dating someone. On one of my Holiday trips home, during an "oh dear, you're still single" intervention, she recommended (strongly) I increase my interest in golf. Not that the sport is so enjoyable, but it is a well accepted activity for men (remember my "date" with Duke Alum?). In fact, as I heard, G-O-L-F used to stand for "gentlemen only, ladies forbidden." If that's the case, what great odds! What other open activities have that kind of male to female ratio? Head out to the links!

Shameless girlfriends try these things as well (worst case scenario, it'll give you conversation fodder over brunch!):

- It's Just Lunch (dating service)
- Matchmaker
- Friends and family (My mom has hooked me up with a number of different people)
- Golf, tennis and going to the gym

- Cultural clubs (one friend met her guy at a wine club)
- Travel (three different girlfriends met their guys on separate trips to Paris – they stayed in touch and then got married!)

MIY Maybe you only date one person at a time.

Boy oh boy do the girlfriends need convincing on this one! Let's start with a familiar scenario. You meet a new guy. You like him, in fact, he seems great! He could be… the One! So what do you do, Girlfriend? You stop talking to all of the other guys you were seeing and/or communicating with so that you can devote your full attention to this guy. And here's where the troubles begin. You find yourself sitting by the phone waiting for him to call. You check your cell every 15 minutes in case you didn't hear your ringer (even though the phone has been right next to you the whole time – and no, it's not on vibrate). You hold off on making plans for Friday and Saturday night because you want to be available in case he wants to do something with you. He doesn't. Oh, and then when you do go out and meet another guy, you tell him you're "seeing someone." Girlfriend, yes you do. You get so excited about the prospects of this new guy that's lasted more than two dates that you start placing yourself in a monogamous relationship in your mind. Only hitch, he's not there with you!

So many of the girlfriends, as soon as they meet a man they like, start cutting off all other avenues to meeting other men. Girlfriend, you're not married yet! Last I checked, after two dates, unless you were in Vegas, you're still single! You do not give up your autonomy to meet other people until he asks you to. No, he's not going to be intimidated by you going out with other guys. It's not going to scare him off. Actually, to the contrary, it's going to make him more interested. What person doesn't want what's in high demand? What do you think he's saying to himself, "Oh, other guys like her, so she can't possibly be the one I want?" Are you serious? How do you think that Playboy has made so much money over the years? Desirable is desirable Girlfriend!

While I'm writing reality checks, let me add one more thing to the mix. If he doesn't call as often as you want him to or ask you out as often as you would like to go out with him, that is the *number one* sign you need to date more guys. First, he's possibly still seeing someone else, so you should too, or otherwise, you and this guy do not share the same view of relationships. Your preference could be seeing each other twice per week and he could only be available once every other week. That is just how much room he has in his life at the moment. If that doesn't honestly work for you (if you're not being desperate and compromising your Standards), then you should date other people. He might be cool, so don't eliminate him completely. He's just not what you want right now, so don't make him your "guy." Keep him loosely attached as a "friendship in development" and stay focused on your objective of meeting more people. Two dates does not a relationship make.

I've now made it my standard practice to say to any of my girlfriends when they meet a new guy, "Great! Now you need to meet at least another two men immediately!" Why? Because unless it is the rare occasion that you two are completely on the same page, meeting a new guy you like is a Code 10 emergency situation! Girlfriend, if you're not dating anyone else at the time, you are in dire straits. Once the first date is over, if all is going well, immediately shift your focus away to meeting someone else. Head to the nearest bar, website, coffee shop, Laundromat or golf course looking your absolute best! I know this sounds counter-intuitive, but hear me out for a second. If the new guy is cute, smart, cool, decent, and fun, unless he is a recent transplant to your city, chances are he is not completely single. Moreover, the odds that he's as focused as you are on becoming un-single are virtually nil. That means, at the onset, you and he will have different expectations of the appropriate frequency of communication and outings. So, refrain from painting yourself into a corner, keep fishing! Continuing to actively meet guys, especially doing so with increased vigor, will keep you from doing the inevitable disastrous action of starting to fantasize about the future and plugging this guy prematurely into your fantasy. If you set your imagination free, all of a sudden he goes from being the guy that you went out for drinks with twice in July to the guy that could go with you to visit your parents at Thanksgiving. We all do it. But putting too much by way of expectations and focus on a new guy when you're nowhere near mutually agreeing to start a relationship will definitely keep you single. Save yourself the ultimate despair and disappointment and more importantly, from him thinking you're crazy. You think the "c" word is harsh? Girlfriend, being crazy is being the only one living in your reality. If you just met a guy and the only person in your relationship with him is you, I'm not gonna *say* crazy… but that word is definitely somewhere in the atmosphere!

MIY Maybe you haven't put equal focus on finding someone as you have on your career and education.

Now, back to "Career-erella." My overachieving Girlfriend, isn't the whole process of school and finding a job a demanding one? How much time and focus do we put into preparing ourselves to enter the workforce! No wonder we're single! Especially if we don't put equal time and focus into preparing ourselves to be in a relationship.

I don't know if you've gotten the memo, but relationships take work. Because it's considered such a natural part of life, we don't realize what that actually means in practice. You study for over 12 years to graduate from high school. That's countless hours and hours devoted to books and homework. Then you spend months evaluating and applying to the various colleges of your choice. Let's not even talk about grad school. When you're finally ready for a job, you submit application after application and prepare for interviews all in the hopes that you land the position of your dreams. Where does a similar type of work ethic come in when you're ready to get involved with a guy? Girlfriend, if we're being honest here, it doesn't! The desire to be in a relationship comes naturally, but the tools to successfully accomplish that objective do not. There's no preparation for a relationship other than actually being in one. There is no perfect substitute for the trials and cumbersome errors that teach us what to do and what not to do, what we like and what we do not like. At this rate, it will take you a lifetime of failed relationships to get it right! So, what's the solution? To fast forward the learning process, you have to benefit from the collective experience of other people! You have to talk and read and reflect. If you want to know more about relationships without having to suffer through the innumerable breakups, read about them! Girlfriend, I've always thought that books were the most invaluable resource we have. Where else can you go to get the benefit of a summary of the collected views and opinions of likely thousands of people neatly compiled in an easily accessible tome of a few hundred pages?

Just like doing your homework and preparing for school, you also need to prepare for successful dating. If only that were a course in high school or college! Don't think it's just going to come to you. We're all learning, Girlfriend, but you have to at least acknowledge that it is an active process rather than a passive one. The passive route takes forever, literally, and it's keeping you single. Just like school is meant to incorporate a lifetime's worth of experience into your little adolescent brain, you must develop a relationship curriculum for yourself. Like you studied in school and applied for jobs, use similar energy to actively find ways of meeting guys. The world is a big place. People are scattered. Your guy might be around the corner and the two of you might never meet. Don't leave everything to time and fate. Time and fate are literally on their own time, and that's a schedule you may not like.

Unless you want to meet your guy when your other girlfriends are becoming grandmothers, you need to get a little proactive. One of the best ways of doing that is to start reading (or listening to) books on the subject. Not just any books, Girlfriend, but good books. Of course I wouldn't just put that statement out there and then leave you hanging, so in the back of this book, I've given you a list of some of what I've read by my own election, along with other titles based on recommendations from various trusted people along the way. You don't have to read all of them, but not reading any of them might just keep you single!

MIY Maybe you think your career will keep you satisfied.

I have a very brave, beautiful and generally fabulous girlfriend who recently quit her job, and even more, her diva-esque career in fashion. This woman with an Ivy-League MBA, who speaks two languages fluently and has traveled all over the world setting up high-fashion retail stores gave it all up because she had a very important realization. One day, explaining her decision to me over drinks and tapas she said, "I know Nikki, it sounds wonderful, but the reality is that I cannot go to bed with my career at night. I need someone, a man, in my life and this type of lifestyle is just not going to allow it." Of course, as a career woman myself, I thought, "She can't be serious!" But I would soon see that she was. About 6 weeks later, I received word that she had, in fact, quit her job and was traveling abroad for an extended vacation. While she was there, she reconnected with an old friend, and having the luxury of not having to return right away, she was able to extend her trip even longer and managed to cultivate a romantic relationship. While she ultimately decided she didn't want to make another country her home, she returned to the US and started her own fitness business, really putting that MBA to good use. Changing her career around to something that now works for her has been invaluable in her dating experiences, as she has already had at least one meaningful relationship as she continues her quest (now with a bunch more time to focus) of finding her "One."

Oh my career-driven Girlfriend, at some point, you're going to have to do as my other girlfriend did and step back to take inventory of your life. You've kept your head down in the books, achieving academically and then professionally. Now, you've got this great career that's rewarding in and of itself, but is that all you want? Truth be told, the answer to that question could very well be yes. I have another fabulous girlfriend who recently told me that at 45 years old, with her interesting and rewarding career and all of her travels, she's not really concerned at all about meeting a male companion and is perfectly content in the event that he never shows up. If that's you, Girlfriend, then more power to you. At least you know who you are and what you want. But, if you've never even thought about it, then you've got some thinking to do. Don't let the decision get made for you when you look up from your all-consuming career at 41 and then start wondering what else there is to life. Save yourself the potential angst of realizing that you really did want the husband and the kids when you're a sneeze away from the end of your reproductive years.

I know this is against the grain conversation, but at a certain point, we Girlfriends have to start realizing that if we are going to try to *have it all*, it takes a careful balance of timing, prioritization and planning to pull it off. You have to know when is the right time in your life to change your focus. Our generation of women has been taught career first, family second. And it was that indoctrination that was intended to give us more options and an increased shot at happiness. Well, if you've got your career and it's your predominate focus, are you happy going at the rest of your life alone? Not alone meaning friends and family, but alone meaning without a mate or a spouse. Give yourself permission to at least wonder if this career track is what you really desire. Don't get so caught up with what you're supposed to want that you miss the bus on what is going to make you happy.

Otherwise, you risk winding up like so many women who grow old, lonely and bitter with all of the things money can buy and nothing that it can't.

Open your mind to thinking your career is not your life. I remember another conversation I had with my same fantastic "I'm happy being single" globe-trotting girlfriend I mentioned earlier. We worked in the same company and this conversation occurred when we had just received word that we were all being laid off. She was so upset because her position at the company had been her dream job. To this statement, I asked her one simple question, "This may be your dream job, but are you living your dream life?" Sometimes, Girlfriend, the two are not one and the same.

Another girlfriend told me of her relationship woes and how had she been willing to move with a previous boyfriend to a different city, she would be married now. Instead, she continues her "career" that is leaving her increasingly dissatisfied as she dates loser after loser in the hopes that she might again find her guy. Chances are she will find someone again, but if she is not willing to compromise some of the things that would hold her back from making a life with another person, then she might find herself telling the same story of her missed love all over again.

You don't have to quit your job to find love or in some way become less of the person you've worked so hard to become. But, you may have to compromise. And, you just might find greater success and fulfillment in the process. Sometimes the best career paths aren't exactly a straight shot. You have to find sideroads and detours to get you to the same place.

If you're going to have it all, so begins a delicate dance in which every part is interdependent on the other. First you have to find the time to get out and meet people. Meeting people necessitates finding the time to date. If you tell a guy that you have no time for him because you're focused on your career, then why should he make time for you? Everyone has to set a priority for what they want. A relationship is no different.

If you think, even for one second, that your career is not going to be all you need to get by during the rest of the years of your life, take a pause for a second and start to reevaluate. Are you working 80 hours or more a week? Are you in a job that has you stuck in one geographic place and not open to relocation? Are you dependent on your wages so much that you couldn't take a brief period off? Girlfriend, you might need to put yourself into career rehab! Working 80 hours a week does not leave you open to meeting new people because you're probably so emotionally and physically exhausted you just can't make it out of your home, that is, when you finally do get home. If you live in a city with a "low coupling quotient" as I like to call it (a couple to population ratio), and you have to stay there for your job or career, you might just be selling yourself short.

It's easy to get caught up in thinking you're setting women back 50 years by prioritizing making a family. Girlfriend, *real power* is being free to be whoever you truly are and to pursue whatever it is that makes *you* happy, whether that is family, career or *both*!

MIY Maybe you put too much focus on spending time with your girlfriends.

I know you love your girlfriends, and Lord knows I love mine, but they may be keeping you single. It's hard to even fathom this point because it's your girlfriends that know you the best; they're the ones that cheer you up when you're down, dust you off, and pick you back up when you fall in love and break your heart. Your girlfriends are the people that you go shopping with, travel with, learn from, and grow alongside. They are your favorite and most comfortable place to be. Still, despite all of the bountiful wonderfulness your girlfriends bring into your life, they are not creating a romantic relationship for you.

Having your girlfriends is an automatic safety net. For the most part, this is a good thing. You should have friends and people to go out and share interests and experiences with whether or not you're in a relationship. The issue arises when you don't begin to re-prioritize when you want certain romantic situations in your life to change. We've all heard the definition of insanity as continuing to do the same thing and expecting a different result. So, while you will never stop loving your girlfriends, and by all means, keep hanging out, you have to realize that something has to give.

Realistically, when you're single, the time spent with your girlfriends may involve shopping, sipping on some fabulous elixir of delightful tipsiness or embarking on a new adventure, but the majority of that time is spent either talking about the boy you like, talking about meeting a boy you like, talking about the boy that likes you or talking about the boy that you want to like you. Let's just be honest here. And while this is fun, while you're talking about the boy, you are not spending time with him or spending time meeting him. One way or another, proper allocation of your already limited time is how your relationship gets cultivated. Constantly turning to your girlfriends for your social outlet keeps you in a comfort zone that doesn't force you to reach outward to meet new people. Believe it or not, the most available person is the one who is alone, not grouped in a gaggle of giggling girlfriends. So, don't be afraid to head out by yourself and get in the world! It's ok to eat by yourself. In fact, that empty seat just invites company to join you.

If you do meet someone, another girlfriend hiccup is the dreaded "girlfriend guilt" you inevitably feel when you begin a new relationship and your other single girlfriends are still single. Listen, unless you want to be single too, you're going to have to get over it. True girlfriends should be happy for you. Scratch that, they should be *ecstatic* for you. They should be pushing you to spend less time with them and more time with your guy. They should look at you as a beacon of hope for them meeting someone in the near future. Believe me, your girlfriends can find ways to occupy themselves that don't involve you. You are not wrong for breaking away from the crew to spend time establishing and developing your relationship. It is a natural progression. And, if things do fall apart with your guy, your girlfriends should be right there for you to help pick up the pieces. That's what real girlfriends do for one another. Not play the guilt symphony every time you are not available for them because you're dating.

That said, this is not – absolutely not – a license to completely abandon your relationships with your friends. There's a careful balance to be had, though unfortunately, it really is rocket science. It's something that you're going to have to experiment with and be honest and aware about. Your girlfriends are a part of who you are and should remain in your life. Just when you want to date or are dating, they can't comprise the predominate focus of your social interaction.

Heading out for drinks with your girlfriends is a great time and should be done often. That said, when you're dating, every night of every weekend is not often, that's excessive. If you haven't met someone yet, start making space in your life. I know it's hard to drag yourself away from your girls, and who wants to be alone when they don't have to be, but give it a try. Go out on your own for a drink or for coffee or for a meal. Eventually, that extra chair may become filled with a new guy! When it does, you've already started working yourself out of the habit of spending all of your time with your friends and set aside some of the time necessary for a relationship. If you are dating, maintaining your friendships is important, but so is maintaining your relationship. Make sure that you're getting maximum social stimulation from your guy (meaning you're spending as much time with him as he wants to spend with you) and rely on your girlfriends to understand as you try to find the right balance. When it's their time to be in a relationship, you do the same for them!

MIY Maybe you don't spend enough time with your platonic male friends.

I once heard this story about a beggar who sat on the side of the road on a box. As people passed by, this beggar asked for money and received enough meager scraps over time to get by and survive. One day, the beggar asked a particular passerby for money. The passerby refused, but before he left, he asked the beggar, "By the way, what's in that box you're sitting on?" The beggar said, "You know what, I don't know. It's just an old box that I've been using for years and years as a seat." At the insistence of the passerby, the beggar opened the box to see what actually was inside. Shockingly, the inside of the box was filled with gold. Girlfriend, if you are not making the most of your relationships with your platonic male friends, you're the beggar, and they're the gold in the box.

Your male friends can be your sounding board, your wingmen (much better than wingwomen, by the way) and possibly your dating pool when you start looking for something more serious. While still friendships, there are no romantic stakes, so don't forget that your guy friends are still guys! They speak "Man," a language you, Girlfriend, do not. Because you are friends, they will be more prone to take the extra time required to make the translation for you. Also, when you ask them for feedback on your thoughts and ideas, male friends can be honest with you as someone who has your best interests at heart, but also knows what's realistic to expect from the male kingdom. And let's talk about heading out to local meeting spots, Girlfriend.

Why are you not taking a guy along? You can't tell me you think it's preferable to a potentially datable guy to see you out with your girlfriends looking like just another single woman in the crowd. Reduce competition when you go out, don't increase it!

Another purpose of male friends is serving as an excellent measure of the floor you should set for how you are treated in romantic relationships. Accepting that the base of all lasting healthy relationships is friendship, if your man-friend can't step up to the same plate as your guy-friends, then you've got a dud who is wasting your time.

Last but not least, there's the so-called "no man's land" of dating your male friends. Listen, Girlfriend, "dating" your male friends should be relationship-lite. It should be what you do when you're not really dating anyone to stay in the habit of relating to men. There's nothing wrong with going on a "friend date" to the movies or dinner or for a stroll in the park. You and your guy friend get to know each other and, in the process, you might see more there that could open up to a new relationship possibility. I admit, this is definitely the danger zone so don't push things beyond their natural course. In other words, no hooking up! Like time with the girlfriends, it's a delicate balance, and honesty will keep you on the right side of the fence. Last but not least, maintain open lines of communication at all times. If you're not feeling something, be clear that you're just cultivating a friendship, not a romantic relationship. Just remember, "friends with benefits" only benefits the guy. You, it's keeping single!

Male friendships are the best thing since sliced bread. Sometimes, all you need is some male energy in your life to get you out of the "I'm single" funk. Your guy friend can also be a much better wingperson for you when you're out meeting people. He makes you seem desired, at least just from first appearances. Additionally, he can keep things light on the approach if there's a guy you're interested in meeting. If your first encounter is more casual, with the aid and intervention of another guy, you'll have a lower-stakes opportunity to get to know your new find before you reach the number-exchange crossroads. Finally, your guy friends have other guy friends! Why waste a valuable entrée into a network of like-minded potentially eligible men? If you don't have guy friends, Girlfriend, that could be keeping you single!

If You're Not Dating Anyone, Maybe It's You...

MIY Maybe you think that all men are dogs.

Girlfriend, all men are not dogs, just like all women are not… well, you know the word! Some are, yes, but on balance, all people, men and women, span the spectrum between good and bad and most fall somewhere in-between. If you start out thinking men are supposed to behave like animals, why even date?

When we go out, it's easy to identify my "all men are dogs" girlfriends by the way they are scrunched up in the corner, focused on their drink with the clear disdain they feel emitting low-grade hate-waves to every man that passes by. Yeah, she's *real* approachable. Girlfriend, don't let this be you! With the popular refrain of man bashing these days it's easy to join the chorus and sing the highest note. Misery does love company. But that negativity doesn't just run off into the atmosphere never to be seen or heard from again; it stays right with you and burrows in your subconscious with the only purpose of coloring your thoughts to pessimistic every time a potential mate does come along.

Relationships, and all interaction for that matter, are a two-way street. The whole purpose of this book is to give you the opportunity to take back some of the power in dating that we girlfriends give away every time we put the blame for our dating failures on something so simple as "men suck." If that's a fundamental truth of life, what is there to do about it? Nothing. What's ultimately more hopeful, and thankfully closer to the truth is, a lot of times, you weren't a perfect angel in the situation either. Know that more often than not, there are thoughts and behaviors you exhibit that may lend themselves to you meeting the "dog" rather than the "prince." *Some* men are dogs, Girlfriend, but if all the men you meet are dogs, maybe it's you.

Girlfriend to Girlfriend

SUGGESTION

Don't always look for and expect the bad in a person. At worse, let them start from a blank slate and show you who they are. I understand the need to protect yourself, but you might just be protecting yourself from Mr. Right without even giving him a fair shot. At best, give a guy the benefit of the doubt (within reason, of course) without you making any assumptions. And stay out of the chorus of complaining girlfriends. I know you want to vent, and it is good therapy, but once you get on that slippery slope, the ultimate landing spot of pure negativity is hard to avoid. (See "Maybe you are unhappy," above.) You don't have to be the voice of advocacy for men, but you have to hold on to your hope whatever that takes.

MIY Maybe you think all dogs are men.

I'm sure you're thinking, "In one breath she says, 'Give 'em a shot,' and in the next she says, 'Whoa, every man isn't worthy!'" That is what I'm saying, Girlfriend! On the other side of the spectrum from my "all men are dogs" girlfriends sit the "well, you can't judge" girlfriends. This type of girlfriend will go out and literally pick up the mangiest stray "manimal" and bring him directly into her house and most certainly into her bed. Yuck! Girlfriend, if this is you, as my grandmother would say, Lord have mercy! You cannot, I repeat, cannot, operate in the world with *no* Standards. Every man does not deserve equal chance in your life. You cannot give everyone full benefit of the doubt! This may sound harsh, but people do not wind up in their current situation entirely by accident. They are there as a result of their choices and circumstances. Everyone deserves a second and third and fourth chance to make it in life, but they don't necessarily deserve to have you in the process.

If I haven't said it before (and I think I have), you are FABULOUS! So, as the incredible wunder-diva you are, you cannot afford to set yourself amongst the dregs of mankind hoping to make a king out of a leper. Unfortunately, if he looks, seems and acts like a loser, he probably is one! Don't waste your time or your divatude on it. I have one girlfriend who is with a guy who didn't have a job when she met him, didn't have a job at any point during the four plus years that she dated him, and still doesn't have a job now. Why would this girlfriend seem surprised that her man still isn't working? Even though he's said otherwise, his actions have been consistent the entire time! In the South, they have a saying, "it's show and prove time," meaning the time for talking is over and now, you must act. Use this approach on the characters you meet begging you to give them a chance. Make a man "show and prove" he can live up to the potential he's promising you before you let him within 25 feet of your front door. If you're dealing with a man on the basis of "potential" then be extra-cautious about letting him into the inner circle of your life until at least some of that potential gets realized. Don't sell yourself short, Girlfriend!

Let's say you find a stray animal on the street. Let's, just for the sake of analogy call it, say... a dog. It's the cutest little scruffy dog you ever did see. He looks up at you with his little pitiful doggy eyes and just begs you to take him home and love him to redemption. I mean, if not for you, he'd go straight to the pound, right? Who else could love that mangy, lovelorn street dog but you – fleas and all. So you decide you're going to adopt that dog and you bring him home. Are you going to hose him off and drop him straight into your bed the first night you find him? Hell no, Girlfriend! You are not. You are going to take that cute little fleabag straight to the vet to get a check-up. You're going to have the vet run every single possible test and make sure you get rid of the fleas, worms and any other thing that dog could have picked up living on the street. You're going to test his temperament to make sure he doesn't bite you when you try to feed him. Now, I'm guessing it doesn't take that much imagination to see where I'm going with this little scenario as applied to a man. If you come across a guy who falls far below your regular Standards, you need to give him the human version of the "stray" treatment. Air him out a bit before you let him into your world. Maybe give him the benefit of the doubt, but do it at a distance. Talk to your girlfriends about it. If you don't want to talk to your girlfriends about it, then if you're honest with yourself, that probably means you know you're really scraping the bottom of the barrel and you don't want the reality check. Wasting time with stray manimals will keep you single, Girlfriend!

MIY Maybe you are focused on the wrong qualities in a man.

One of my girlfriends told me she won't date a guy that doesn't have a six-pack. Funny thing, moments later in the conversation we began talking about the last guy she dated who was so immature that not only did he not know how to treat her generally, he virtually stood her up on their last Valentine's Day together. Yes, this girlfriend is still single.

Girlfriend, by all means set Standards, but you should be realistic about what qualities normally do not come packaged together. Most SUV's aren't usually available as convertibles, are they? There's a reason for that. In similar fashion, certain types of men that you might be lusting after just don't come with the "act right" package. For example? Let's say you are obsessed with your guy having the body of a Greek god and the face of an angel. If we can agree that looks are generally the first basis for attraction between people, then how many other women might spring for this same guy if they happened to see him? Do you think he would ever have trouble meeting women? Probably not. Meeting the shy, "I'm really just a computer geek who cleans up well" is a fantasy only alive in the Superman franchise. Odds are, if that guy is spending that many hours in the gym, he wants a return on his investment of blood, sweat, time and tears. Most likely, Girlfriend, that return is not you. Well, not just you. Maybe you plus a couple of others, so if you don't mind, you're all set. Have you ever worked out hard in the gym? Like really hard? If never, I suggest you do so at least once. Then, take that experience and multiply it by 3 to 5 times per week, every week, *ad infinitum.* What do you get? You get half of the work your super-buff Adonis has to put into his regimen to achieve the physical results that make you salivate. The other half of the equation? Alimentary deprivation. That means, a careful diet not only lower in calories but lower in all the yummy things that can make you fluffy. That's the price of a hard body. Name me one person that pays such a hefty price for no return. You can be in denial if you want to, but that guy wants heavy payback. He wants attention and he wants lots of it.

Anytime you become too fixated on any single characteristic of a guy, you lose the opportunity to strike the right balance between the qualities that truly work for you. As we discussed in "Maybe you don't know what you want," you should expand the focus of what you're looking for from singular descriptions (tall, rich, hot body, *etc.*) to descriptions of how this man makes you feel. This allows you to evaluate the whole person, rather than just a walking collection of individual traits. When you concentrate on the effect (on you) rather than what you think could be the cause (*e.g.*, you think a hot body will make you feel sexually attracted to him) then you miss out on all the men that might be deceptively right for you, but can't be identified because you're caught up with trying to compare him to a list of irrelevant characteristics.

Girlfriend, maybe the physically, mentally, spiritually, ethically and financially perfect specimen of a man exists, but the reality is you're probably not going to meet him first. So, play a game with better odds and look for the man that is physically, mentally, spiritually, ethically and financially perfect for *you*! How do you find that person? Stop focusing on superficial characteristics and start digging into the whole package. You might just be pleasantly surprised!

MIY Maybe you keep picking men who want to be single (and will tell you if you ask).

One unexpected thing an ex told me is loosely paraphrased in the following: a man is really not going to tell you anything that he doesn't want you to know. This means, if a guy tells you he's not looking for anything serious, he's serious! He's serious about not wanting to date *you*, Girlfriend, and you should take him at his word. See, sometimes we as the wonderful women we are think we are the exception, rather than the rule. Unfortunately, if you got to this point with your guy, where he's telling you he doesn't want anything serious, or worse, if he's telling you about *some other girl he's dating*, you've already reached no man's land. That's when it's time to pull out the girlfriend to girlfriend megaphone and tell you "*STEP AWAY FROM THE GUY WHO DOESN'T LIKE YOU!... STEP AWAY FROM THE GUY WHO DOESN'T LIKE YOU!... Please head to the nearest graceful exit from the relationship that is <u>not</u> going to happen.*" If a guy didn't want something serious when he met you, and you changed his mind, you would never know. Number one, he'd have never told you he wasn't looking for anything and number two, he would have worked the entire situation out near instantaneously. Don't sell yourself short Girlfriend!

Now, I know this will sound like common sense to some, but believe me, I've had a number of my more stubborn girlfriends-in-denial argue this next point into oblivion. If you too have doubts about the above, it is probably based on the following thought: "But at least he's being honest with me. I'm glad he told me he's dating other people. I'm dating other people too." Or, even worse, "I'm happy he's not looking for anything serious. Neither am I! I'm just having fun." Ugh! Girlfriend, the man version of "dating other people" and "I'm not looking for anything serious" is *absolutely nothing like* the female version. One hundred eighty degrees of different. The man version of "I'm not looking for anything serious" means he's not even looking to remember your name, and if he does, it's probably because you're doing something for him that he likes. The problem is he's never going to care about what *you* like. Never. Not at all. And, it's not going to matter to him. Why? Well, he told you: HE WANTS TO BE SINGLE!

When you rush to the defense of a man that is treating you like you don't matter with the rationale of "well, I'm looking at him like that too," there are only two things at play here: (1) You are in a denial so deep that catfish are swimming past or (2) You are just plain wrong. When a guy doesn't care about you, he really doesn't care. It's not like he doesn't care that much or he only cares a little. He doesn't care *at all*. When a man wants to be single, it means that he wants to be *selfish*.

A WORD ABOUT *single men...*

It's not just the guys that tell you they want to be single that fall into the category we're talking about here. It's also the guys that want to be single because of their own circumstances. Guys that fall into this category are usually those pursuing a financial or career goal, dealing with some personal issues or are between jobs and can't meet the financial burden of being part of a relationship. These guys are just generally looking to avoid the ties that might bind them to another person to prevent bringing about additional responsibility they're not ready for. You should avoid these men as well. Not treat them like lepers, but that's not far off.

The best thing I can do for you here, Girlfriend, is to identify signs and signals – some obvious, some not – that let you know that even though a guy is acknowledging you, he really wants to be single, or at minimum, he just doesn't want to date you. Eliminate the denial, and start focusing your attention on someone else!

Hey, Girlfriend! CHECK THIS OUT

Signs That He Wants to Be Single

(or is just not really interested in dating you)

1. He tells you that he's not looking for anything serious (or utters any similar statement).
2. He tells you about any other woman that he's dating.
3. He says that he's not looking for a relationship (yes, he actually means that).
4. He doesn't call you.
5. He says that he doesn't want a girlfriend (hopefully, you're starting to get the point).
6. He has never made plans to see you before 8 PM (…and don't make excuses for him here).
7. He says he just wants to keep things "light" (Girlfriend, you are not a diet beverage…).
8. He doesn't ask you questions about yourself.
9. He says that he's not ready to date anyone right now, just have fun (the point should be coming into sharper focus now…)
10. Your primary activity is sex.

MIY Maybe you don't take the right guy seriously.

My guy friends tell me all about what they call the "nerd's revenge" that ultimately happens later in life. Many of my eligible, successful, handsome, and generally stellar single male friends are straight dogs at this stage of our lives. Why? Because they can be! But really, because they were all but ignored growing up as they dug deep into their books and studies to make the grades that would ultimately lead to their now enviable careers and accomplishments. But we wanted bad boys then, right Girlfriend? We wanted that guy that could give us a sense of danger and excitement. The guy that made us feel like we were the special one that could "tame" him and bring him indoors to our fantasy wonderland.

Girlfriend, you are a grown woman now, and continued pursuit of the bad boy will keep you single. You do not have time to tame a wild animal. You have a job, a life, and goals of your own. You need someone who is going to support you in making the most of yourself and who wants you to support them in maximizing themselves. The bad boy just wants to be bad. It is a losing game to want a guy that is nice only to you. If being nice is not in his true nature, his real self will show sooner than later. Stop fooling yourself into thinking you're the exception. How hard would your eyes roll if one of your girlfriends told you, "yes, I know he's cheated on all of his past girlfriends, but I know I'm different. He definitely won't cheat on me." Ugh! If he kicks small furry animals when he walks by, it is not because he is just waiting for you to come into his life to make him a nice person. He's just a jackass. Leave him alone! He's keeping you single.

Another thing to remember, financial security is not the same thing as emotional security. Sure, Girlfriend, let's be real, you feel better if a guy is taking care of you financially, but a "sugar daddy" is not a substitute for your real dad. So, don't make your financial "needs" outweigh all of your other needs, including your emotional ones. Possibly even more than always going for the bad boy, always going for the "rich boy" will keep you single as well. Who is meeting your emotional requirements? They're still there. You can't pretend they're not. Your wealthy man will read that as being too needy and then there you are, my platinum-digging Girlfriend, single, yet again.

If you're still craving the exciting thrill of a bad boy and you want a serious relationship at the same time, unless you change what you're looking for, expect to be single for a while. When you get tired of having your heart shattered and crushed underfoot, start looking for the guy that is just generally a good person and treats all people in his life well. Odds are, worst case scenario, he'll treat you well too. Best case scenario, you really are the exception and he treats you even better. I don't know about you Girlfriend, but those sound like winning odds to me.

MIY Maybe you can't get the sex thing right.

This is an area where so many girlfriends drive the relationship right off the cliff. Girlfriend, if you can't get the sex thing right, it may be keeping you single. First off, based on all of my research, *no one* has said your own personal morals and values, if honestly held, are keeping you from a relationship. That's just pure crap we women make up. You do not need to sleep with a guy in order for him to date you or to like you. And, possibly more surprising, you do not need to abstain from sleeping with a guy you like in order for him to date you or like you. Essentially, Girlfriend, the sex thing is not about him, it's really about *you*.

A girlfriend deciding to engage in sex with a guy has what I describe as "the Pricetag." Now, I know your mouth is open and you're thinking, WHAT?! Is she calling me a prostitute? No, I'm not. Not at all. The Pricetag is the set of expectations you attach to having sex with a man. The theory of the Pricetag means, in *dating*, there is really no such thing as "no-strings attached." No strings is truly *no strings*, and that is a one night stand. If you're dating a guy and you're expecting a relationship to form, Girlfriend, hate to break it to you, but there is a Pricetag. So many of the girlfriends go into situations thinking that they are just going to "do it" and then go with the flow. These are the same girlfriends that are upset he doesn't call afterwards, or waits too long to call, or even worse, when they see him out with another woman. These situations only arise when you have sex before you're sure your Pricetag will be covered.

So, what is *your* Pricetag? It could be that you expect him to call you the next day, or you expect him to sleep over, or you expect that after sex, the relationship is now monogamous. It could be anything and you should not feel like you're wrong for having those expectations. Girlfriend, your Pricetag, like your Standards, is what ensures you're going to feel ok at the end of the day. It's your protector. So, if you're not going to feel ok if he doesn't call you the next day, if he's not calling you virtually every day before you sleep with him, then you better hold off until he is. Sex is not going to change the landscape of your relationship. Not one bit. In fact, you can assume that if you have sex with your guy for the first time on Saturday, whatever happened on Friday will be exactly what will happen on Sunday. Sex just isn't the game-changer we all expect it to be.

Another thing Girlfriend, don't think you have to change who you are if you meet a guy that you think has real potential. He probably already knows what you're like and doesn't care. If you're naturally a party-girl, he didn't pick you in the hopes that you'll become a librarian. He picked you for who he already perceived you to be and that's cool. If you think you need to change your sexual behavior, take a dating time-out and do that yourself, don't try to do it on the fly with a new guy. That's just asking for a dating disaster.

A WORD ABOUT *the Representative...*

Girlfriend, the "Representative" is what I call the guy you first encounter when you meet your guy. Please do not be confused thinking the "him" that you initially meet is the real *him. Odds are, it is not. The guy who's doing everything right, that's his Representative; and, that Representative is only going to make it for about the first 90 days. After that period, whatever façade that guy has been putting up to try to get what he wants from you gets dropped. That's when the Representative leaves – and introduces you to the* real *guy you're dealing with. You don't even know what you have until you spend about 60-90 days with him. It's the Representative that gets so many of the girlfriends into trouble, and it's gotten me on a number of occasions. Everything was so great and then all of a sudden, he just flipped a 180 and turned into a freakin' manimal with no warning whatsoever. Then you find yourself wasting valuable time and emotional energy hoping he'll change back. But Girlfriend, the real guy has already stepped in and he's showing you who he is. There's no going back. Absent some epic movie plot-type disaster, people don't start off good and then suddenly turn bad. This behavior is classic Representative departure. And please don't sit there racking your brain trying to think of what you did. You didn't do anything. Really, you didn't. You did nothing at all. He didn't change. You didn't change. He's simply stopped pretending. So, when it's the Representative's time to leave, he leaves; without any pomp, circumstance or announcement. That sudden shift in your guy's behavior early on into the relationship is just his Representative walking off the job and make no mistake about it, once his stay is over, he is* never *coming back.*

The moral of the story is be true to yourself and your Pricetag. Don't change up the sex timeline just because you think someone is going to form an opinion of you one way or another. If you sleep with a guy and he stops calling you, he was dating you just to get to the sex and what do you want with him anyway? The only way to get around that is to string him along to make sure you get a glimpse of the real person after his Representative leaves. If your Pricetag is being met after 90 days, then maybe you can feel more confident that your Pricetag will continue to be met after you engage with the "naughty torpedo." That said, I've heard plenty of stories of married and engaged couples whose sex timeline is literally all over the map. I've talked to couples who slept together the first night and are still together after 3 years, having barely spent a night apart since and couples who waited a few weeks that eventually got married and are still together going on 10 years later. Bottom line, you have to be honest with yourself and the situation. Of course, it also wouldn't hurt to have a conversation with your guy to make sure that you're on the same page about whether or not he's willing to meet the terms of your Pricetag.

MIY Maybe you're trying to "take things slow."

Every time I meet a new guy, my single girlfriends tell me one thing, without fail, "Make sure you take it slow." I can be an impulsive wreck, so if there is one thing I'm incapable of, it's taking things slow. For that reason, most of my relationships are quick intense flashes and then over. Yes, I also wear my heart on my sleeve, so for a brief period, I am completely devastated when the relationship ends. Moping, ice cream, 15 pounds of weight gain, the whole nine yards. But, eventually, I lose the weight, raise my spirits and quickly meet someone new. It was something I always felt guilty about – meeting a guy and letting that relationship spark ignite. All of a sudden we're going from zero to sixty down the relationship highway. I like this pace, Girlfriend. It keeps everything 100 percent honest. Sure, it also keeps me in the danger zone, but you know what else it does, it shows me what I'm really dealing with right away. Intensity is one thing that will make the Representative disappear.

It's like pushing the relationship fast forward button. That means I waste as little time as possible with Mr. Wrong. So, I thought that I was just being weak and over-indulgent with no discipline… until… I started talking to married people.

Girlfriend, while there are some married people who evolved over time as a couple, there are many who said that one way or another, when it was the right person, they pretty much knew right away. Relationships, when the two of you are on the same page, have a certain momentum. That's something you don't want to take lightly and certainly not waste. That means, if the natural flow is to see each other every day, don't start making up some arbitrary rule that you should only see each other once a week in the name of "taking it slow." While I prefer to put advice in black and white, the honest truth here is that this is more of a gray area that you're going to have to feel your way through. Unfortunately there's no rule of engagement (no pun intended). To try to give some kind of standard, while your guy wants to see you or talk to you as much as or more than you want to speak to or see him, you're in the "don't take it slow" zone. If you find that you want to talk to or see him more than he wants you, you're in the "danger, date other people immediately" zone. If you're in the "don't take it slow" zone, don't waste the relationship momentum. True feelings don't burn out. They only grow. Well-lit fires get bigger when you *feed* the flames, not starve them. If the fire was poorly lit with little material to burn in the first place, it's going to burn out quickly. Consider the materials to burn in this relationship the things you have in common, including your views on relationships, what you're looking for in another person, as well as the things you both like to do.

Girlfriend, there is a very thin line between a situation where you should not deliberately take things slow and the situation where you should pump the brakes. Here's another guide. If your action is to slow yourself down because you're moving quicker than the pace of the relationship, yes, you're right to lift your foot off of the gas. But, if you're trying to slow the relationship down artificially because it's moving faster than you *think* you should move, then you're likely keeping yourself single. To be clear, I am specifying "moving faster than you think that you should move," meaning you would otherwise want to move at that pace but for one reason or another (including fear of getting hurt), you hold yourself back. In this case, get out of your own way!

MIY Maybe you're playing too hard to get.

You should be easy to find, not so easy to get. That should not translate to impossible to get. That's not the plan here, Girlfriend! If you find that you are meeting a lot of men, but dating no one, then playing too hard to get could be the culprit. If you're doing either of the following, including setting impossible Standards or requirements, or making your man jump through more hoops than an acrobat, you could be keeping yourself single!

One very important thing… you are a prize. Absolutely, but that doesn't mean you need to be purchased. Please do not set a financial floor to your affections. Yes, your guy should take the lead role in pursuing you, but that does not necessarily involve buying you diamonds for your birthday and Louboutins "just because." Cut him some slack. He should come to you correct, but that doesn't mean that he has to be or have everything perfect. If you're constantly focused on what he didn't do, rather than what he did do, then Girlfriend, you may literally be pricing yourself out of the dating market.

Girlfriend to Girlfriend SUGGESTION

If no one is meeting your Standards, try putting a pause on dating and approach your interaction with new people from the perspective of building a friendship. That means treat him and evaluate him exactly as you would a friend. Meet for coffee, and go Dutch when you go out. Or, trade off paying for each other, just like you would do with one of your girlfriends. Use this opportunity to figure out what it is that you really need from another person. Who knows, one of those "friends" might turn into something more!

MIY Maybe you're too demanding.

Girlfriend, there are women that are too hard to get, and then there are those that are too hard to stay with. Both, are single. Finding yourself in a relationship is not your license to give up all of the responsibilities that maintain your own being. Expecting another person to take over for you in covering your basics just because they are there, is the seed of complete and total misery. Your guy is not an extension of you, supposed to pick up and do all of the things that you don't feel like doing. Make no mistake, you shouldn't be that for him either.

Imagine your guy has a hobby, let's say karate. And after every karate class, he brings his dirty, nasty, sweaty karate clothes over to your house and drops them in the middle of your floor to then go about his business with the expectation that you will see the clothes there, pick them up and launder them for him. Sound ridiculous that someone would dump their responsibilities in your lap? Well, Girlfriend, it's just as ridiculous to expect your guy to pick up your slack. Don't get me wrong, in a relationship, both people should look out for each other and have each other's back, so to speak. Going too far means expecting someone to live your life for you. That's being unreasonable. What's the extension of that Girlfriend? How do you know if you're being too demanding? Well, that's easy. If you're being too demanding, you're blurring the line between expectation and appreciation. To illustrate, think of how you feel when your guy gives you a gift. You're appreciative right? You get gifts and show appreciation because it was something that your guy didn't have to do. Both of you are on the same page about that. Expectations are a horse of a different color. Expectations are requirements. If expectations are not met, that comes along with a negative consequence. So if you expect your guy to spend Friday night with you and he doesn't, then he's in the dog house right? When you turn something that you should have appreciation for, something that should not be a requirement, into a requirement, that's when you become too demanding and annoying. Being too demanding and annoying keeps you single. To name a few situations and circumstances:

Hey, Girlfriend! CHECK THIS OUT

Are You So Demanding and Annoying It's Keeping You Single? You could be, if:

You don't have a stable financial situation on your own and you expect your guy to buy you the things that you can't afford. Notice I say "expect." Gifts are nice, but those are unexpected bonuses.

You don't clean your house (or car) and expect your guy to do that for you.

You require your guy to give you his precise coordinates and schedule, rather than just spending time together.

You insist on accompanying your guy everywhere, rather than giving him some space.

Don't turn your guy off with unnecessary requirements!

Girlfriend to Girlfriend

SUGGESTION

Girlfriend, please don't take the foregoing to mean that your guy shouldn't do things for you. That's not true at all. This describes what you shouldn't *expect*, meaning, there shouldn't be a negative repercussion coming from you if he doesn't deliver. To the contrary, your focus should be on positive reinforcement by way of showing appreciation and giving him thanks. If you're dating instead of setting your own goals, living your life and handling your own business because you expect that a man will do that for you, then you better look like the lovechild of Halle Berry, Angelina Jolie and Eva Mendes, mixed with a little Giselle for good measure. Unless you're planning on becoming a supermodel overnight, be content with making some easy changes that will keep you from running off the men that want you for you (rather than just for what you look like).

MIY Maybe you think that ignorance is bliss (and don't ask questions).

I have a wonderful and very sweet girlfriend who has been dating a guy that she likes for about two months. They get along great when they're together and she thinks he's smart, sexy and very attractive. All that said, there are a few things about him, or better, what he does, that give her the slightest pause. First, he never calls her. I don't mean that he calls only once in a while. I mean never, like not at all. He only communicates with her via electronic means (Facebook, text message, IM, etc.). Second, there's no regularity to their going out. She'd like to see him more, but he doesn't seem to be available. I know that you have to be familiar with this scenario, Girlfriend! I certainly am. This same thing happened to me, and I wondered what was going on until I ran into him at a concert… with his girlfriend! I am not telling you this to encourage you to start making assumptions. Assumptions are bad little demon-like creatures that, once set loose, take on a life of their own and destroy your relationship. Trust me, you want nothing to do with them. No, this is about finding the courage to ask direct questions and being prepared for the answers. What point is there in constantly asking your girlfriends and the guy friends that you haven't run off already to play oracle and try to guess "what he's thinking" or "what he's doing" instead of calling you. If you want to know, it is useless, absolutely useless to ask your friends. *They* don't know. Only the guy knows.

So anything you're doing besides asking him directly is a maddening waste of time. It's also keeping you single. Answering the question that's bouncing around in your head gives you the benefit of certainty and certainty allows you to adjust your behavior and expectations.

There was a period in time when I decided the first question to ask any guy that I considered dating was "are you dating other people?" Previously, it seemed so unnecessary. I mean, why would he be out with me if he had someone already? Then, came the string of men that I later (after many tears and "why isn't he calling" conversations) found out either had girlfriends that they didn't tell me about (because I didn't ask) or some other serious kind of situation that made the dating field we were playing on less than equal. In fact, not so long ago I met a man at a mixer. He asked me for my number, and called me the same night to see if I was available to meet for lunch the next day. I thought that he was such a charming gentleman! As it turned out, I had to cancel our lunch plans. When I tried to reschedule for later in the weekend, he told me that he was going out of town and I never heard from him again. I soon found out, based on invaluable information from one of the girlfriends, that this guy was married! And he was never actually headed out of town; he was using the time that his wife was away to try to slip in a quick one with a woman who didn't ask questions.

Girlfriend, there is nothing wrong with making a direct inquiry of your guy from the outset. Asking him if he is seeing anyone else is not a statement to him that you expect the answer to be no. It's just a question for relevant information. It is a mistake to assume just because he's out with you he doesn't have someone else at home. Assumptions will have you knee deep in a relationship only to find out three months later he has a wife and children. At least if you asked, he'd have to lie to deceive you, rather than you just living in ignorant bliss.

If you and your guy mutually decide to progress your relationship to something more established and serious, you should really feel free to ask anything. You can't later blame him if you didn't do the minimum on your end of trying to find the answer. Most importantly, you need to identify the best timing to Define the Relationship ("DTR"). The moment to DTR is the very second you know for certain what you want. Otherwise, you risk not being on the same page. Not being on the same page with your guy means certain doom for your relationship. Again, it sets the stage for uneven expectations and assumptions. This is the stuff that legendary breakups are made of. Do not be afraid to DTR. Like I said before, ignorance is absolutely not bliss. It is the path to pain and heartache when, after six months, you find out that he wasn't looking for anything serious, and all the while you were thinking he was "the One."

In the case of dating, ignorance is never bliss! What you don't know is *exactly* what will hurt you. It's only fair for you to ask pertinent questions. You don't need to get a credit score on the first date, but you do need to know what you should expect going forward. But, if you don't inquire, he's not going to offer up the information. Number one, he's not going to tell you what he doesn't want you to know; number two, he doesn't think it's relevant; and number three, he assumes that you don't care because you didn't ask.

What questions are necessary and appropriate? I've included a few examples and grouped them based on when they should come up. If you're afraid to ask, Girlfriend, chances are you're floating down the river of denial without a raft! Grab yourself a lifeline and get on solid ground with your guy!

On first or second date:

- Are you dating anyone right now?
- What are you looking for? Friendship, relationship?
- How long ago did your last relationship end?
- Do you have any children?
- Where do you work?

Before sex:

- Are you sleeping with anyone else?
- Do you have an STD?
- Are you heterosexual?

A WORD ABOUT *the way you ask questions...*

Ok Girlfriend, there is a way to ask questions and a way not to ask questions. Because I know how we can be, I feel the need to point this out. It is not a question if it ends with "didn't you?" That is an accusation. Also, it is not a question if it starts with "isn't it true that" – that is a statement. To ask a question, I mean really ask a question, you have to approach it from the perspective of not knowing the answer in advance. Then, the question is fair.

Make sure that you don't turn asking questions into a way to keep yourself single!

MIY Maybe you don't say what you want, think or feel.

One of my girlfriends, in telling me about her guy, described how she wanted him to do certain things for her, but she felt strange about asking. Girlfriend, don't be afraid to ask for what you want! If you want a long-term committed relationship, why not say that up front? It's not going to help if you try the sneak attack four months down the road. If you do know for certain what you want, don't feel like you can't share that immediately with your guy! Another girlfriend, on the first date with her husband, told him, "I want to get married and have children. I am dating to meet my husband." Her husband, who tells this story to anyone who will listen said, "Well, that's good to know. You've got the wrong guy." So, then Girlfriend, one dinner between them turned into two which turned into three and so on. They decided that since they were not on the same page initially, they would just have fun together as friends and take the pressure off of their relationship turning into a romance. How did they wind up married after the initial brush-off?

Expressing her wants made the playing field even. With no hidden agendas, the two of them were free to get to know each other casually and found that they really enjoyed each other's company - so much so that they eventually did decide to date. And, when they did, he already knew what her expectations were and he was prepared to step up to them. As the most important "bonus," their friendship was so strong that they decided they should spend the rest of their lives together.

Are you the Girlfriend that tells guys "No, I don't want anything serious" after he tells you he's not ready for a relationship, in the hopes that after a certain period of hanging out and "free" sex, he'll eventually change his mind? If so, that's keeping you single. You're being dishonest about your real needs and intentions. Eventually, resentment accumulates and there's an ultimate emotional explosion where, in built-up frustration, you spew your love-guts all over your unsuspecting guy. He's wondering, "Why are you so angry?" And you really don't have a reason, do you Girlfriend? All you know is that you're pissed! Well, I'm telling you now that in this situation, you're mad because: (1) your plan didn't work, and (2) now you've likely lost any possibility of maintaining the friendship as well. Do not make the mistake of falsely communicating your needs, wants or feelings to your guy just to match what he's told you he wants or is feeling. This is the seed of disaster. Having sex with him is not going to change his mind. What it will do, however, is create more of a bond for you and prevent you from meeting *other guys* that *are* interested. Eventually, when you finally get up the nerve to tell him you do want something more after all, he's going to look at you like you're crazy and one way or another, your feelings will get hurt. Stop this from happening from the beginning.

True enough, the start of a relationship is a "no mans land" period and you may not actually know where you want to head. With nothing invested, you really could just be trying to figure everything out about this new guy and situation. If this is truly the case, so be it Girlfriend, explore away. However, the second that you know what you want – and this means, you have that relationship pang, then it is time to "DTR." If you don't know what he wants, you are in trouble. You're leaving yourself open to travel a long way down an unidentified road with no map, only to find yourself at the edge of a steep cliff. Don't waste your time. Sure it's scary to face being alone again now that you've found someone, but it's even worse to find yourself in a one-sided relationship going nowhere while you've wasted the time you could have spent meeting someone else. Someone else who actually wants the same kind of relationship you want, that is.

What are you afraid of my uncommunicative Girlfriend? Do you think he is going to have a negative reaction if you tell him what it is that you actually want and need? To avoid what you perceive as "confrontation," you just want to take your chances with him reading your mind? I don't know if anyone has ever told you this before, and if not, I am honored to be the first: despite popular opinion, men are not mind readers. If you think that they remotely know what you want, think, or feel in any way without you telling them, you're giving them way too much credit. In fact, any semblance of them even coming close was just pure dumb blind luck. If you *do* say what you want, what is the worst that can happen? He'll balk and walk away? Ok, so then what Girlfriend? Now you know he can't (or won't) accommodate your needs. So, at least you are free to meet and greet with someone who might be able to give you what you want and you've wasted little to no time on the guy that couldn't. On the other side of the consequences for speaking your mind, best case scenario, the guy actually does like you and is willing to make a few modifications to make sure that you're happy.

Stop worrying about whether or not expressing your thoughts, opinion, wants or feelings is going to scare a guy off. Do you really believe relationships are that fragile? Building a relationship as a house of cards is building a relationship that is going to fall eventually and quickly. Tell your guy what you want the very minute that you know. Give him an opportunity to respond in words and in action. If the response is unfavorable, then that's great! That means you know right away that you need to conserve your efforts and place your focus elsewhere. Time not wasted is time well spent! If you don't express your wants, needs and feelings, then you're stuck with what you've got and really, the fault is your own.

MIY Maybe you spend time nagging and complaining.

Girlfriend, we talked about this a bit in "Maybe you're selfish" but it's so important, it's worthy of being said twice. You and your guy do not speak the same language! You don't think the same way; you don't interpret things the same way. You may look at an apple and think, fruit to eat, he may look at an apple and think apple juice. There's no telling. For that reason, you cannot make assumptions based on what you would think, do or feel if in a similar situation. That leads to an inevitable waste of your emotional energy. If your guy isn't doing something (*e.g.*, doesn't take out the trash or doesn't invite you to outings with his friends) why are you going to complain to him about it?

Let's really get to the nitty gritty of nagging and complaining. What is it? Girlfriend, if you're brave enough to admit it, nagging and complaining is your sub-conscious attempt to impart your *own* negative feelings about something that your guy is or isn't doing *to your guy*. Think about it for a second. Your guy doesn't invite you out with him and his friends. You're pissed because you think that the lack of invite is inconsiderate and is him "hiding you" in some way. So, you start complaining, telling him that you can't believe he would do that and how thoughtless it is and the like. All the while to him you're sounding like wah wah wah. How dare he ignore your feelings you say! Well, my whiny Girlfriend, here's the real deal. Decide if you're looking to find a solution and actually solve the problem, or if you're really looking only to transfer your negative energy so that he feels as bad as you do. Be honest.

I'm sure that you've done this at least once in your life to another person, be it male or female. That person did something that made you upset. So now, you're angry, but they did it, and they're just going along with their life like nothing's wrong. They're fine! But, you, my furious Girlfriend, are not. You are not fine at all. So, what are you going to do? You're going to give them a piece of your mind. You're going to call them up and tell them exactly how you feel. And you're going to be hostile about it too 'cause you are pisssssssssed! Stop. Stop right there. Now, thinking about that exact moment, right before you're about to pick up the phone, how are you feeling? What are your thoughts and what is your intention? Is it to find a solution? No, not at all. You just want to unload! On top of that, you want to unload with such hostility that you ensure they feel the full impact of how their action made you feel. So, at the end of this conversation, do you expect that person to be in a good, chipper mood? Hell no! You expect that they'll be closer to your own sulky wastelands! Well, guess what, Girlfriend? You keep doing that and unless they're related to you, that person is going to start avoiding you like the plague. Let me tell you why. Nine times out of ten, if he did something offensive to you, he was completely oblivious about the effects of his action. This means that he had no intention to hurt you or your feelings. If he didn't intend to do it, then you can't rightly blame him for it. He only can (and should) control his intentions.

In contrast, harmful effects sometimes can't be controlled, especially when they weren't intended. Let me give you another example. When you were a kid, let's say you were washing dishes, and you reached up to put a plate away and it slipped and fell to the ground and broke. You had been doing everything that you were supposed to, but in that one instance, an accident happened. Let's also say that unbeknownst to you, that plate happened to be number eight in your mother's prized china collection. Now she's down to seven and that plate isn't available anymore. Your mother finds out and is extra-mad. You find yourself on punishment for three weeks and can't go to the Homecoming dance. Is that fair? I would say no Girlfriend! You didn't mean to break any plates, and certainly didn't know how important that particular broken plate was. So understand why it's not really fair to unload on your guy when he unintentionally does something that makes you mad. If you really want to be effective and stay on good terms, then you must always look to find the solution. And this doesn't mean going to your guy every time he does something wrong and saying "What's the solution?" That's annoying. Looking to find the solution should be your reason for doing the things you do, asking the questions you ask and making the statements you make.

A solution avoids assumptions and starts with objective fact gathering. He doesn't think with the same brain that you do, so try for a second to suspend judgment. If the offense is something that he repeatedly does, then figure out if letting him know how you feel has actually made a difference in his behavior. If he's really present in the relationship, it should. If he knows that something bothers you and either: (1) he can't explain it so that it makes sense for you, or (2) he doesn't modify the offending behavior, or at minimum make a real attempt, you have a problem. And, to be clear, it's a problem that nagging and complaining is not going to solve.

Now, the reality is that some of the girlfriends like to nag and complain. It gives them a way to increase the flow of hot air through their body systems. It gives them something to talk to their mothers about on the phone. If that's you, then just be honest about it… and, of course, realize that it's probably keeping you single.

Girlfriend, stop wasting all of your emotional energy in a way that can yield no positive results! If you're nagging and complaining, chances are, if he hasn't packed his bags already, then he's just learned how to tune you out. When something happens that you don't like, or doesn't happen in the way that you want it to, be honest with yourself about your real intention in addressing the situation with your guy. If you're at an emotional peak, like right after some triggering event, you're most likely simply making a transfer of your negative emotion to him. If so, nothing is going to get solved. Step back and take some time away to think about the situation from a "solution wanted" perspective, then give yourself more time and energy to determine what is the optimal solution. Tell him your preference. Remember Girlfriend, you can only tell him "what," you cannot tell him "how." Telling him "how" is annoying. Annoying = No Ring. Get it?

MIY Maybe you're carrying baggage from old relationships.

Is it possible to be in two relationships at once and not realize it? Most of the girlfriends are. It is an entirely common occurrence to date a guy, while constantly living that experience through the lingering memory of past relationships. Past relationships can mean with other men that you've dated, or non-romantic relationships with family members, most commonly your Dad, whether he was present in your life or not.

Girlfriend, in fact, your relationship with your Dad, or other father figure in your life is your first relationship with a guy and lays the groundwork for how you view relationships to come. If you can't come to each new situation with fresh eyes, heart and mind, then Girlfriend, your baggage is likely keeping you single!

We all have baggage. Elimination of the taint of old experiences is one of the hardest things for a person to do. I know for me it is. Past experiences serve us by giving a framework to make educated guesses about future experiences without having to do the work of actually going through them. With this past experience in the back of mind, you're actually unintentionally acting as if it's still true.

If you think all men will leave you, you're not investing in any relationship what you would if you expected your guy to stay. In your mind this is a temporary thing and so, being treated as temporary, the guy eventually goes away and your history again becomes your present. You cannot cheat on your current guy with all the guys that you've dated in the past. Think you're not, Girlfriend? Well, if you're still carrying the baggage, then on some level, you're still in that relationship, at least in your mind.

If you don't think you're carrying baggage, try this little experiment. The next time your guy does something you don't like, stop yourself in the moment that you begin making your doomsday predictions. Ask yourself, ok, am I thinking that this is the beginning of the end because of something he has affirmatively told me, something that I'm basing off of past experience with him specifically, or something I'm basing off of past experiences with someone else? Pay attention to your thoughts. If you're thinking in any way, "Well, when (insert name of third-party) did this, that meant he was going to do X, so that must mean my guy is about to do X." Girlfriend, you're doing the baggage thing.

Give your guy the benefit of the doubt enough to let him establish his own pattern before you start judging. If this is too hard, and you're too inclined to protect yourself based on past relationships, then slow down the dating and exist as friends. This will allow you to keep enough distance to just observe without feeling like your emotional well-being is at risk. Let every new relationship stand on its own Girlfriend, as just what it is, a new relationship!

If You're Not Married Yet, Maybe It's You...

MIY Maybe you aren't your own person.

If I haven't said it before (and I'm pretty sure I have by now), you are FABULOUS! It's your own unique brand of fabulous that made your guy interested in the first place. If he wanted something different, he would have picked a different person. To that end, don't let him have a better understanding of your core being than you do. If you don't clearly know who you are, and that includes: your Standards; your likes and dislikes; your goals and ambitions; your sense of humor, and your ethics, morals and spiritual view; amongst other things, then you're like an unanchored ship in the ocean! All of this collection of wonderful habits, ideas, and preferences – that is what makes you interesting. Almost every man that I've asked what they're looking for in a woman said that they want someone who has their own interests and goals. Getting into a relationship is not the point to stop your self-development. The purpose was not to do just enough to get someone and then the party stops. A guy wants a girl who's got her own party going on and whose party *doesn't stop* once they get together.

Like a lot of the girlfriends, we get a guy and on the one hand, we're so relieved to be with someone, and on the other hand, we're scared to lose him; so we stop doing what we used to like doing, including that which gave us our identity. This approach most certainly leads only to one place… you guessed it, being single! You've got to do the upgrade on yourself based on who you are and what *you* want, not who or what you perceive *him* to want. If a guy buys a '57 Chevy, he wants a '57 Chevy. While he wouldn't mind if he woke up one morning to find it fully-restored to its original condition, he most certainly would mind if he woke up to find a 2007 Chevrolet in its place. The guy that picked you, he recognized your individual traits at the outset and is willing to take them for a test drive, as long as you stay the same "car." Now, Girlfriend, this does not mean that you should avoid the upgrade. If there's something you can improve, and of course there is, then tackle it. We all should be constantly striving to become the best possible versions of ourselves. All that said though, you don't want to unintentionally pull the bait and switch and wind up making the biggest dating mistake ever!

Being in a relationship doesn't mean that all things you enjoy should automatically stop. Before you pump the brakes on all of your social activities, friends and pursuit of your goals, ask yourself if it is really necessary for the relationship to be successful. Ask your guy what he wants instead of assuming based on past experience. Plus, if you're busy being you, you won't have time to notice when he's not calling or the time that passes when you're not together. The more interesting and unique you are, the more he'll enjoy you when he can get you!

MIY Maybe you're lazy.

Dating takes work, Girlfriend! Lots of it. One day you're struggling to find time to make it to your job, the gym and drinks with the girls, and the next you're racing out of work, running down the isles of the grocery store to grab what you need for dinner to make it home and get everything ready before your guy gets there at 8. Does this sound far fetched? It shouldn't. This was me in the third week of dating my ex. He had treated me so well in the previous weeks that I thought it was definitely time for me to reciprocate with a home-cooked meal. The only problem? I work long hours and since the dinner plans had been somewhat last minute, I had no time to prepare! Originally, I intended to write down the ingredients that I needed from my neat little cookbook and take my neat little list to get what I needed and head home. What actually happened was a time crunch so severe that I found myself clutching my *Rachael Ray 30 Minute Meal* cookbook to my chest in the supermarket while I played grocery cart wheelies trying to grab all of my ingredients off the shelf while reading directly from the recipe on page 244. Did I make it home in time? No, not really, but I did manage to pull it all together at a respectable hour for dinner. My lesson in all of this? Just the basics of being in a relationship are enough to move you far beyond your routine and normal comfort zone. You're going to have to clean, cook, keep yourself up, listen to his stories, go out, stay in, make the bed, straighten your bedroom and bathroom and just generally modify your routine. You're going to have to balance your work schedule, your gym schedule and your guy schedule, not to mention friends and family, and make it all happen. To successfully accomplish all of this, you cannot be lazy. Not one little bit.

Like the common cold, "the Lazy" can affect even the most energetic girlfriend once she starts getting too comfortable in her relationship. How do you know if you've come down with the Lazy, Girlfriend? Often, signs and symptoms take a slow progression that goes unnoticed until, one day, you just have the full-blown disorder! Lazy means that you're exhausted from work, so you just don't take the extra 10 minutes to fix your hair and throw on some lipstick. Lazy means that you're too tired for sex, so you're just not able to find a way to entertain your partner's desires. Lazy means that you don't feel like putting in the extra work to accommodate another person in your life, and so, you just don't do it. If this is you, Girlfriend, and you're always too tired, too busy or too *lazy*, then you need to rearrange some things in your life so that you're left with more energy for your guy.

Girlfriends afflicted with another, equally virulent strain of the Lazy, rather than fix the problems in their own lives, expect a man to come in and fix them. Bad credit? A girlfriend with the Lazy, rather than taking control of her finances would look to her guy to pay her bills and co-sign for the next thing she can't afford. You can't expect a guy to deliver you to the lifestyle that you can't provide for yourself Girlfriend! Sure, it happens, but everything under the sun has its price. Most men are not looking to be your caretaker and provider where you fail to be that for yourself. Guys want a true partner. Someone that is stable on her own two feet which allows the two of them to travel further together than each individual on his or her own.

Avoid the Lazy like a plague.

While the Lazy is perfectly common to contract, the cure is simple. Start making time to do things for yourself. If you're single and dating no one, focus on what you'd expect to do in a relationship so that it is already part of your routine. Don't wait. If you're already in a relationship and not doing what you'd expect to do in a marriage, incorporate those actions one at a time. You'll find that you have more energy and desire to spare if you don't focus on the entire "to-do list" all at once. Remember that you're involved with another person whose desires, needs, and perceptions do not dissolve just because one or both of you now feel comfortable in your relationship. They want the same woman they started with! And, most importantly Girlfriend, take care of *yourself*! Make sure that your own bases are covered and that you're as complete as possible before you invite someone else to form a partnership. If your basics aren't met (financial stability, living situation and transportation, personal upkeep and grooming), then you're really not in the best position to present yourself to someone else for dating or marriage purposes. You need to take a time out and repair the potholes in your life. If your relationship with yourself is bad, there's no man in the world that can fix it for you.

MIY Maybe you don't cook.

Ok, I know that none of the girlfriends is Betty Crocker, but that doesn't mean cooking for a man is not still important. Surprisingly or not, in my surveys, and in my experience, cooking is still a significant factor to men. Why? Because even with times as they are, with everyone being so busy, growing up, your guy most likely got his food in some way from his mom, or the "mother" figure in his life. Maybe she (or he) didn't cook, but nonetheless made the food appear and all your guy had to do was show up at the table and eat it. Traditional gender role or not, that food experience was a big part of your guy's first encounter with feminine love. Even with a time crunch, one thing that is never going to change is our need to eat. And beyond simple nourishment, food is a language; it's an expression of care and comfort, not to mention, if well-prepared, sensual indulgence.

Ok Girlfriend, I know that you might still be balking at even the suggestion that you need to cook to have a husband. I mean, you're educated, you work, you're busy, you're interesting and you keep yourself up. Why the need to cook? Well, as I said before, because he needs to eat! Sometimes it is just that simple. Cooking is a good way to provide him something that he'll definitely want and need and it's a great way to express who you are. Do you need to cook dinner every night? Hell no, Girlfriend! Hell-to-the-no! Like you and I both said, no one is Ms. Crocker. But, cooking can be an activity that you organize, just like he may organize inviting you out to dinner. It's your show, so show yourself off!

Girlfriend to Girlfriend

SUGGESTION

I know that times are hard all the way around and it might even seem near impossible to figure out not just what or how to cook, but also how to find the time. Look, one of my good girlfriends told me, "If I'm not serving it to him in the package it came in, then that should count for something," and she couldn't be more right. Guys don't really care how much time you spent on it, or even really where it came from. Just the ease of not having to go anywhere, to sit right down at the table and enjoy some (hopefully delicious) nourishment is a great experience itself! Don't slave in the kitchen! Use pre-prepared products to your advantage!

Pick a time, maybe once a week, or once every other week, that you do cook. Don't pick a set day, because you may need the flexibility to change things around if you get busy. As you start feeling more adventurous, experiment with basic cookbooks. I know 30 Minute Meals got me through and still does! Find what works for you and have fun!

Don't be afraid of the kitchen, Girlfriend! Think of it as your dating workbench!

Hey, Girlfriend! CHECK THIS OUT

Shortcuts to Homemade

Trader Joe's has great pre-cooked meatballs and spaghetti (in the frozen section) for a wonderful Italian dinner.

Trader Joe's also has delicious Indian food that is shelf-stable. You can even pick up pre-cooked rice!

Pre-seasoned roasted chicken can be purchased at nearly any supermarket or **Sam's Club**.

Glory Foods has fantastic-tasting pre-prepared canned southern comfort food if you want to save 2 hours cooking greens and black eyed peas.

Marie Callender also has yummy-fabulous pies, ready to bake so you can have delicious smells coming from your oven when he gets there!

MIY Maybe you don't clean…

Oh Girlfriend, my Girlfriend. I know that you must be thinking – "Is she serious? Who has time for cleaning?" Well, if you don't want to be single, that person is going to have to be you. Have you ever heard the saying "cleanliness is next to Godliness?" Well, I'm going to switch it up a little and say cleanliness is next to goddessness. There is nothing more off-putting to a man than a woman's unkempt environment. I can't even begin to tell you of the countless stories that men of all ages have told me about their experiences with a woman keeping a dirty home. For men, it goes back to that mother thing, and their first experience with feminine love. Now, Girlfriend, if your schedule is anything like mine, you are certainly busy. But again, to move out of your single lifestyle, certain things about the way that you have been living are going to have to change. One of those things is making sure that your home is not just clean enough for you, but it is also clean enough for a perfect stranger to feel comfortable and assured that you're taking care of business on your end. You don't have to do his laundry or clean *his* place, just ensure that *yours* is looking sparkling when he gets there.

I remember hearing a story that one of my guy friends told me about a woman that he had been seeing. They had gone out a few times and this particular instance was his first time coming over to her home. As soon as he stepped a foot in the door, he was ready to turn around. There were dishes in the sink and the bathroom was a disaster. Girlfriend! If you clean nothing else, clean your kitchen and your bathroom. Those are the two places that, if dirty, would be the dirtiest and most obviously dirty. They also happen to be two of the most likely places your guy is going to visit. Well, that is, until he's allowed in your bedroom. So, if you have limited time, focus on those two areas first. In order, I would say bathroom then kitchen. Don't miss the little corners and crevices that dirt and buildup can hide in (especially behind the knobs of your bathroom faucet and behind the toilet). If you don't think he'd notice, make no mistake, if he's considering dating you, and *especially* if he's thinking about marriage, he's checking it out.

If he's worth it and you really don't have the time or inclination, hire a maid to come in for an hour to clean. Have her focus specifically on your kitchen and bathroom and let her help you get it extra-super clean. Then, try to do quick upkeep on a regular basis so that you don't find yourself in need of the massive overhaul every time you're expecting company.

MIY Maybe you co-habitate.

I used to think that living together was no big deal. To date I've never done it, but I have been one in the past to "innocently" leave a toothbrush or even "feminine products" behind at my guy's place. If I do have any trepidation at all about co-habitating, it stems largely from the refrain of my mother and grandmother saying over and over again "Why buy the cow if you can have the milk for free." That, I understand. But, an equally compelling thought – living together is so much more cost effective and you want to know what you're getting into down the road, right? Wrong. You know what changed my mind? All of the many conversations with married people. Almost every married person that I've asked, either in casual conversation, interviews, or via surveys has said that if you are not married, you should not co-habitate. Their rationale is akin to the cow analogy, but different. Vastly different. Married people say, "Why buy the cow if you can have the cow and the milk for free, you don't like the cow and the milk's not that great?" What does this mean, my co-habitating Girlfriend? The cow represents responsibility, which if brought on too quickly could very well doom your burgeoning relationship. If you move in together too soon into your journey together, your guy will want to give the cow back, immediately.

A married friend told me the following about co-habitation, loosely interpreted, "Relationships are impossible; that's why if you want to stay in one, it needs to be impossible to get out of it. That's why marriage was invented – 'til death do you part, sometimes the other option doesn't seem so bad."

Girlfriend, when you first meet your guy, you are a complete mystery; an incredible creature of mystical delights. You magically appear in his world, make-up perfect, clothes impeccable and smelling great. There's no sign of the cosmetics containers that you left strewn around your bathroom, the ironing board sitting in the middle of your bedroom or your rancid gym clothes balled up in the corner. It's just you, walking in wherever being amazing. He's shielded from all the work that it takes to get you there. Now, your guy isn't an idiot. He knows that you need to get ready and that your healthy body is not by accident. That said, it's not the first thing on his mind when he sees you. To him, you're just simply gorgeous and well put-together. In that moment, that's all you are. Why would you not want to preserve the dating glow as long as you can? That's one of the benefits of living apart. You can control how much he sees. He may think that he's ready to have *all* of you, but then again, he hasn't seen (or smelled, ew!) you after you get back from the gym!

A WORD ABOUT *personal space...*

I'm not saying that you should forever keep your true self hidden from your guy. What I am saying is shield your relationship from some of the things that are solely your responsibility until it's really time to put all of the cards on the table. You've got a lot of positives, Girlfriend! Why overwhelm him with the negatives before he has time to unearth all the good stuff! Use your personal space to your advantage!

Before you go running over there to drop a toothbrush, let me just say this. Every relationship is not going to lead to marriage. So, don't be in such a rush to make it look like one. I know that you want to see your guy all the time if you can, but honestly, leave some back for him to discover! Don't hurry to lay it all on him all at once to see how he "deals with it." Let him get used to your little quirks over time, where they become part of the bigger picture rather than an overwhelming glaring neon sign in the middle of an otherwise picturesque landscape. Keep your mystery as long as you possibly can. When the two of you start talking about a real commitment, like thinking of marriage, he's ready to assume more of your drawbacks. So *then*, Girlfriend, start letting him more and more into your world.

MIY Maybe you are focusing on the relationship you want, rather than the person you're with.

My self-sufficient Girlfriend, isn't it nice to be able to put in a little bit of work and get whatever it is that you want in life? Unfortunately in relationships, certain things are outside of your control. As a woman, we find ourselves a slave to our biology. Whether we like it or not, when that clock starts ticking, it's like a ringing alarm in our ears! Many of the girlfriends decide at some point either, "I'm going to *now* be in a long term relationship," or even worse, "I'm ready to get married *now*." And so it starts, the frantic, mad dash search for "the One." Some of the girlfriends luck up and find the right guy just about the time that their patience is set to run to empty. Other of the girlfriends, well, they simply settle. Remember our happy little soldiers, the Standards? Girlfriend, if you start prioritizing the type of relationship that you want (*e.g.*, MARRIAGE) over the person you're with, your Standards are in big big trouble. You're dropping them off to battle with no equipment and no exit strategy. They're doomed for destruction.

If you find yourself with a guy and your clock is ticking down, whether that clock is biological or otherwise, understandably, you might very much want this guy to be "the One." You've put so much time and effort into the relationship, so what if there are a few **GLARING** problems because he doesn't meet several of your core and basic Standards. You can't help who you love, right? Girlfriend, that is so right. You 100% cannot help who you love. Love is a marvelous thing that only comes around every so often. How wonderful it is. When you fall in love, watch out, it's a powerful drug. But guess what, while you cannot help who you trounce off into the magical love garden with, you can absolutely 100% choose who you marry. Marriage is not a helpless process. Marriage is a decision, and love is only one of the many prerequisites to making that decision. But love is not the only prerequisite, and that is why you have Standards, that is, if any have survived the attack of your ticking bomb timer. Your Standards should be what determine if this is a person that you can make a life with or not. If you become desperate for a relationship or desperate to marry, you run the danger of sacrificing your most fundamental requirements. And Girlfriend, believe it or not, if you don't let your Standards go to work keeping away the stray dogs in life, eventually your Standards will turn on you. What does this mean? It means that in the back of your mind, if you do stay with this sub-par guy, the things that bothered you in the beginning, like the fact that he didn't meet your Standards, will continue to bother you and either make you crazy, make you miserable, or make you… you guessed it, single.

It is the most likely, by a long shot, that your guy is not going to change. If he seems lazy, he is lazy. If it looks like he lacks ambition, he does. If he's a cheater, he will continue to cheat. People are who they are. You cannot transfuse a man with potential just because you want him to fit into shoes he can't fill. Girlfriend, you want to get married because that type of relationship is supposed to be a certain way; however, the wedding isn't some magical day that makes all wrongs right. You may get him to the altar, but at the end of the day, you're now just making an even deeper commitment to stay with a guy that doesn't meet your Standards. You may get married, but you're still married to him. He doesn't become your ideal man magically just because he puts on the ring.

Girlfriend to Girlfriend

SUGGESTION

Don't let your desire for a certain type of relationship make you desperate. You are FABULOUS! Remember that! You deserve a man that meets your Standards. A hamburger isn't steak just because you cover it with A1, ok! If you're in a relationship with a man who doesn't meet your Standards, don't move forward until he does. And, give yourself a time limit. Don't stay with that guy forever by thinking no one is going to meet the Standards you set. That is settling and fantastical fantabulous girlfriends don't settle! Girlfriend, if you find that you're dropping Standards just because the guy you're with doesn't meet them, you're going about this the wrong way. That's trying to make the guy fit the situation, rather than letting the situation fit the guy. If he's not marriage material, then Girlfriend, don't even think about marrying him!

MIY Maybe the men you're dating are too young.

If you've ever heard that women mature faster than men, Girlfriend, from every ounce of research I've done, that point is true! I don't know what it is, but if growing up is a train, women are in the conductor's car and men are firmly rooted in the caboose! It's like they mature in reverse dog years! But anyway, I digress.

Let's talk facts and figures. In my dating survey, even as the number of responses has increased, one thing has remained the same. Women in the 18-40 age bracket overwhelmingly rank "dating" and "marriage" as "most important." This remains consistent even when broken up into different age categories (*e.g.*, 28-34, 18-30, or even 34-40). But check this out, when given the same options, men in the 18-40 age bracket choose "career" and "increasing net worth" as "most important" (roughly 65% of respondents picked both of these options). Guess what these men ranked next as "important" – hanging out with other men! Only 34% picked marriage as the "most important" factor. You know when men started to rank marriage and children "most important" over their career? Not until the 40+ age bracket! Seriously, believe it! As the rapper Jay-Z states so effectively in one of his songs, "Men lie, women lie… numbers don't!"

What does this mean for you? It means that prior to being able to focus on permanent or long-term relationships, your potential guy is focused on establishing his financial stability and means of income. While women are able to multitask, serving both masters, as it were, men absolutely are not. And up to a certain age, they're not focused on *dating* you, they're spending their spare time with their friends! Make no mistake, Girlfriend, you and I can agree that it's easier to date within your peer circle. These are the guys that you see most often. But you know what? If you want your best shot at a long term relationship with someone who is placing equal importance on marriage, you better skew your age requirements up a bit. It is unrealistic to think that your 30 year old buddy from school is ready like you are to move into the settled family life. He's just entering into his prime money-making years! He likely just wants to keep it casual and if he does marry you, it will be after years of dating. Younger guys mean longer dating runway. And it's not always because he's still making up his mind about you. Just as much, he's still making up his mind about himself, making sure that he can meet his set financial goals and professional ambitions. So, if you're 30 or 31, and you want to be married by 32, you better be looking for guys closer to 40. If you're ok with dating for a while, and not seriously at that, then by all means, keep it local. Just saying, on the bright side, at least you'll have *plenty* of time to plan and fantasize about your wedding.

Girlfriend to Girlfriend **SUGGESTION**

Girlfriend, this section is really super important. It's crucial because many of the facts that go along with a man's development process are just immutable, set in stone. You can't change them, no matter what you do. So, given that's the case, you better learn how to navigate this landscape because it is full of pitfalls. Here's the real deal. If you are looking to get married sooner than later (like within a year to eighteen months), then your guy search better be hitting 35 and older. If you're ok with the long dating road, then younger guys are fine for you.

If you're in NY or LA, and want the short track to marriage, you need to be focused on men that are even closer to 40, if not older than 40. Why are things different in LA and NY? Because of three things: (1) distractions, (2) cost of living and (3) career potential. People in LA and NY, because of the nature of the industries located there, can and generally do want to ascend higher on the ladder of their chosen professions. Accomplishing those goals takes a longer period of time. Dating distractions just are what they are. Flashing lights, pretty girls, parties and clubs, can take your man's focus quite easily and that means increased competition for his attention. Finally, the cost of living is more in those cities, so your guy has to work even harder and longer to achieve financial stability. For other large cities that are not NY or LA, you can slide the age scale down from 40 as appropriate, depending on the intensity of the three "maturation delayers," distractions, cost of living and career potential. If these are low in your town, then congratulations, you just might be able to relax your age threshold a bit, but with caution, because age is a factor that will certainly cause you to waste your precious dating time Girlfriend!

One more thing about guys and their maturation process. There are many bestselling books explaining how men think, and I won't delve into repetition, but what I will say is if a man does not have his financial stability established, please do yourself the favor and leave him alone. It is not being superficial to set "financial stability" as a Standard. If it makes you feel better, use your own standard for yourself and apply it to him. If you were in the same financial state of affairs, taking into account all factors, including what he is doing to address the situation, would you be satisfied with yourself? Girlfriend, if no, please let that man go and allow him to get himself together! You are fabulous! If you do not, he's going to be dissatisfied and so will you. Don't delude yourself into thinking it doesn't matter, especially if you're looking to have something more permanent and long term. Not matter what you think right now, eventually it will matter and it will make you single!

MIY Maybe you think you can change a man.

My grandmother used to tell me the only thing that you can ever expect a man to change is his shoes. Now that I'm older, I pretty-much believe her. Despite her expert advice, I am guilty of what I call "digging through the crates" meaning that I have been known to circle back to an old relationship every once and a while. I once broke up with a guy because he was unreliable and completely inconsiderate of my feelings. Often in our first round of dating, he would tell me that he was going to do something and just simply not do it. This included standing me up on my birthday. Call me naive, but I usually take people at their word. In his case, that was always a complete mistake. Still, I found him funny, incredibly interesting, attentive when he wanted to be, and cute. So, when the opportunity to rekindle the romance came up five years later, the memories of earlier pain had faded and I was open to the possibility. We decided to meet in Atlanta (I lived in LA at the time and he in DC), and so I happily jumped on the plane. When I got to the hotel, after many hours passed with no sign of or word from him, I eventually realized that he wasn't coming and set about finding some of my friends who lived in the city. I made the best of the weekend, but that old dog certainly was up to his old tricks.

Girlfriend, unfortunately the reality is that most people don't change. The reason is that change is hard. First you have to recognize that there is a problem. If it's not a problem for you personally, and let's face it, most people are selfish, the odds are already low that you'll get past the first step. If you do, then you have to decide that you want to change and finally, actually take steps to change. Steps to change are not an overnight process. There are steps backwards, relapses and the like where sometimes making progress is just standing still. Most guys are immediate gratification junkies. They understand instant rewards and swift repercussions. If the pain of their improper actions doesn't hit them immediately and directly they won't internalize it. So, Girlfriend, if he's making changes just because you asked him to, they won't last. Trust me. He'll say that he's going to do it and make a good and consistent effort to stay on course, but ultimately if he hasn't made a deep personal commitment to the change, he's not going to stick with it.

Girlfriend to Girlfriend SUGGESTION

Take a mental snapshot of the relationship you're in right now. This means, consider everything just as it is, right at this moment. Do not give yourself the benefit of cheating on your guy with his Ifhethen. Look at your guy as he is right now and assume that he will never be any different. This snapshot is your actual relationship. Do you like what you see? Add to that the commitment to be 100% real with yourself. Does that relationship look like what you'd want someone that you care about to be in? If not, why would you accept less for yourself? If I haven't told you before, you are FABULOUS! Fabulous for everything you've worked so hard to become and everything you're working for in the future. Care about you first and best. If your snapshot isn't what you would wish on your closest friend, why on Earth is it ok for you?

And my dear Girlfriend, if you do ignore my advice and opt for the "wait and see" strategy, please believe, a guy changing while you're dating him is about as common as finding a new planet in the Solar System. Just assume that we've pretty much got what we've got. If you think you're dating the 11th planet, why don't you ask him directly his thoughts about what you think he needs to change. See if it's even something he has internalized. Chances are, this might be a rude awakening for you. Girlfriend, change takes action and if your guy isn't taking those steps (and talking about doing it doesn't count) you're a long long way from the relationship promised land.

MIY Maybe you stay in bad relationships too long.

Do you find yourself in a less than ideal relationship past the expiration date? Like milk gone bad, you know when the time is up, but you just have to keep tasting to make sure, absolutely sure that it's sour before you pour it down the sink? Do you try to squeeze in one last bowl of cereal too many? Oh my lingering Girlfriend, why do you do this to yourself? You know this dating situation. You and the guy have been together awhile. He's no longer exciting or excited about you, but you two are comfortable and you've put the time in, so you figure, well, why not stick it out. Maximize what I've got right? Well, Girlfriend, maximizing what you've got means changing something to attempt to obtain the optimal outcome. If you either (1) don't change anything or (2) don't obtain the desired outcome, it's time to bail! Get out! Get out now! Inertia will also keep you single!

Let's be clear about one thing. Marriage, that's the commitment you make to stay together forever no matter what. That's when you've both decided that this relationship is permanent and you're in it for better or for worse. Dating, that's only a commitment to see what this relationship is. It's a commitment to the free trial period, not the full subscription - like the cell phone company letting you use a phone to try out their network for a couple of weeks before agreeing to the year long contract. There are a lot of benefits to having that contract, including a cheaper handset, but in the process of the free trial, if you realize that the model of phone you're using is generally a sucky product, are you going to enter into the contract with the wireless carrier anyway just to get the discount? Hell no Girlfriend! There's no amount of discount that would make you want to *buy* a defective phone! So why do the opposite in relationships? Once you see that you've got a defective guy, if he's not working for the intended purpose, why are you sticking around? Don't sell yourself short! Just because you are dating does not mean that you are under obligation to keep dating. Moreover, once you pretty much know that the relationship is not working, you are not obligated to push a non-working relationship to marriage! What are you doing?

I know what you're thinking. Hopefully, I can change your mind.

Well, if we broke up, I'd be alone and I don't want to be alone.

Girlfriend! Are you serious? Yes, if you are in a monogamous relationship and you break up with your guy, you will be alone... temporarily! If your real concern is that you're not sure who would want you if not him, then let's get to the real issue here. Ok, so maybe right now you're a 5. Then upgrade yourself to a 6. If you can get this guy now, imagine what you can get if you put in a little work. Clearly, this situation is dysfunctional, so you can only do better. Just don't make your dating experience a "race to the bottom," meaning that you set even lower, rather than higher, expectations for future relationships. You should be constantly striving for improvement. Not just for yourself, but improvement of your relationships. If you don't have a situation where you, your guy and your relationship are continually growing and improving, he is not "the One." Bail! Jump out of the plane and pull the rip cord!

I feel bad. If I leave now, then it's like I was just using him until

I could upgrade to something better.

Girlfriend, seriously? Please stop with the pity parade! Your guy is as responsible for creating a good, positive, healthy and constantly progressing relationship as you are! HE should be trying to move things forward and towards the better just as much as, if not more than you! He should be growing as a person just like you should be growing as a person. The relationship should help facilitate that, not hamper it. You are not using him if you're not using him! Using someone is an intentional behavior. If you are actually using him, deliberately and on purpose, that certainly isn't fair. But, if you're in a relationship with him and you've been trying to make it work, it isn't and you come to that realization, you haven't been using him this whole while if you get out of it. You've upheld your end of the bargain. Dating is for making an honest, earnest determination of whether or not a longer term relationship is going to work. The answer doesn't always have to be yes.

He could be "the One." We've put in all this time so far, why wouldn't we stay together?

Everyone is not "the One." Stop injecting potential where it does not exist. Have you ever heard the saying "if 'IF' was a spliff, then we'd all be high?" Girlfriend, stop tokin! If he doesn't seem like the right guy for you and he's not making you feel like you want to feel, let's just call it what it is. Stop trying to make him something he's not. If you're thinking about him and the first thing that comes to your mind is "if he..." followed by anything, he's not the right guy! Chances are, if he hasn't already, he's probably not. Your expectations may lower, your self esteem may plummet, but he's probably not going to ever reach the other side of that "if." Why are you sticking around? Learn the lesson of that relationship, and assuming that he's not going to change, make the honest determination of whether or not it's going to work.

Like I said before, every relationship is not the road to marriage. Most are just detours. That's not harsh, that's the reality that you haven't been considering. Time put in does not make it a marriage. A mutual decision and commitment makes it a marriage. You don't have to say "it's like we're married" if you actually are married. Don't impersonate a commitment on your end that he's been unwilling to make himself. Make no mistake about it, if he hasn't married you yet, he's not sure about you either. That said, why give him the benefit of your unwavering devotion if he hasn't done the same. Dating is not marriage. Dating is not even a commitment to continue dating. Dating is a trial period, an exploration. If you see that either the guy or the relationship is defective, don't go for the long term contract. Just get a new one.

MIY Maybe you're sexually uptight.

Girlfriend, in case you hadn't gotten the widely circulated memo, men like sex. They like it so much that they spend the majority of their time, money and focus either trying to figure out how to get it, trying to get it, thinking about getting it, or actually getting it. The rest of the time in their lives is reserved for… well, things like eating, breathing, working and general life basics that keep them in a position to be able to have more sex. If you don't like sex, that's one thing that you and your guy definitely do not have in common.

Now, if you are a celibate Girlfriend or have otherwise decided that you want to save sex until you're married, that's absolutely, perfectly fine and commendable. It's nice to know they still make you. Stay true to yourself and more power to you as you try to resist the tides of modern day society pushing us all in the opposite direction. Everything that I have to say in this little ditty "Maybe you're sexually uptight" assumes that you are sexually active with men and further, that you have been sexually active with the guy that you're with or that you're usually sexually active when involved in a relationship.

So listen, Girlfriend, if you know he likes sex, why are you rationing? He's your guy already right? You've done it once already right? Why withhold? Surprise or not, in many of the conversations I've had with both men and women, withholding sex came up as one of the most commonly perceived problems that women present in relationships. What are you saving it for? Your virginity does not come back after a long period of non-use of your lady-parts! Really, the more you engage, the more comfortable you become. The more comfortable you are, the better it gets. And believe me Girlfriend, he wants it to be better.

Costumes, whips, chains, handcuffs, poles, stripper heels, stripper classes, does any of this sound familiar to you, or is it offending your delicate sensibilities? Well, just remember my Puritan Girlfriend, there's always another woman who will answer that question with a resounding NO. Sex is everywhere, it's an open market. You can no longer rely on the girlfriends to hold themselves to the same purity-ring standard of the 1950's. The gate is wide open and the beast is loose. I'm not saying that you need to bring Cirque de Soleil into your bedroom (though if you can…), but you better start thinking about switching it up, and quickly because your man's mind is being constantly bombarded with imagery, ideas, concepts, fantasies and the like and you don't want to find yourself struggling to catch up. In the beginning of the relationship, a willingness to even have sex is considered "openness" to new things. But after you've been going at it awhile, your guy wants to see you show and prove that you're still the same woman he started dating. Look, a certain frequency and intensity got you in the relationship in the first place, please don't kid yourself into thinking that a different course of action will keep you in the relationship, or even more unrealistically, get you further down the path. It won't.

A WORD ABOUT *oral sex…*

It's important. They like it, so get over it. It is not a myth; it is not legend; it is not conjecture. It. Is. True. You don't have to make it an everyday occurrence, but you do have to figure out how to make it a part of your sexual routine, safely and comfortably, for the both of you.

Girlfriend to Girlfriend SUGGESTION

If you're not prepared to become an erotic aerialist, that's ok. You don't have to head directly down the rabbit hole with him just yet. There are some strategies that you can use to get yourself more "open," so to speak, to new sexual experiences with your man.

1. Get comfortable with yourself. Learn how to enjoy yourself naked.

2. Peek at porn. It'll give you some ideas. Even better, watch with your guy and find out what he likes.

3. If your guy is into things that you're really not comfortable with, don't tell him no. "No" just makes him want it more and consider it a challenge. Instead, focus more on the things that you are willing to do. Make yourself a wanton sex goddess in your own comfort zone. He might abandon his thoughts of acts you're not into just because he has so much success with what you already do.

MIY Maybe you take advice from single women.

Girlfriend, before you say, "*You're* single and you want us to take advice from *you*!" let me say a few things. In this discussion, where I've given you my opinion (not often), I'm calling it my opinion. That means I'm just telling you what I think based solely off of my experience. So, just based on opinion alone, I only tell you about (1) meeting people and (2) getting into a relationship. Where I give you advice, it is based on literally years and years of research, formal and informal surveys of thousands of people with direct experience and me finding the common denominators to pass along to you, my fantastical fantabulous single Girlfriend. So, let's be clear on this – just because I make a statement as fact does not mean that I'm stating my opinion as a fact. It is the common denominator of gobs and gobs of fascinating research! Ok, now that said, many of your other girlfriends do not operate this way. They will give you advice on dating when they, themselves are single, and that advice is formulated solely based on what they think. This is truly the blind leading the blind. And that is a disaster.

Girlfriend, single women are not your guidepost to being in relationships. Would you ask someone who is off-beat to teach you how to dance? Yet and still, the single girlfriends will always get together and sip and chat about men and relationships. Sooner or later, "What do you think?"

will come out of someone's mouth. If you're looking to get married, Girlfriend, just don't let it be yours. Your single girlfriend's answer to that question will keep you single!

Let's say you want to be a professional basketball player. You have your choice between two people to seek guidance from, the first is your high school teammate and the second is a player on a current NBA roster. The choice is easy right? With dating, it is completely understandable that you want some guidance when you're headed down a path that you've never treaded before. It's also totally natural that you'll turn first to those people closest to you who know you best. Unfortunately, though they may know you, they don't know the subject matter. Girlfriend, you do not need another person to tell you what *you* think. So, for real and effective singlegirl relationship advice, especially when you're trying to get to the altar, look here first: people that have successfully gone down that path before (*i.e.*, married people only).

Why so narrow? Because, Girlfriend, as well-intentioned as they might be, unmarried folks have not successfully reached the ultimate goal of dating, and therefore, cannot give you real and solid advice on how to get there.

If you still need third-party influence, another great source of guidance – books. Knowing a little bit of something about this subject myself I can tell you that writing a good and thorough book takes a lot of time, research, dedication and intelligence. It's quite a process! And for that, it's worth it to get the benefit of someone else's hard work, especially if it is readily available in your local library, bookstore or on Amazon. So, Girlfriend, rather than asking for irrelevant advice, grab a relevant book and read it. Don't know where to start? Check the "For Further Reading" section at the back of this book.

MIY Maybe you share intimate details about your guy with friends and family.

Don't we all love to talk? Especially when we're feeling emotional about our guy, we need to share with the closest person to us. Quite often that's someone who falls into the category of friends and family. If your guy makes you mad, what do you do? You call your mother, best friend, sister or other confidante. But, Girlfriend, do you call this person every time that your guy makes you happy? No, you absolutely do not! So, from the perspective of an outsider, after all that "sharing," your relationship looks like Good: 2, Bad: 32, with your guy playing the ultimate villain jackass that you should get rid of immediately. Now, isn't that a problem!

When you're in the moment and you need to vent, your one-sided story gets firmly imprinted in the mind of the person that you're talking to. So then, when you wonder why everyone hates your guy, look back to all of the things you've said about him in the past and how much they skewed towards the negative. Sure, he's got his good and bad qualities. To you, the good outweighs the bad, but you have the benefit of 100% of the time spent with him in that relationship. No one else saw *all* of the "little things" he did that made you forget about his last transgression. So all that venting you're doing to your friends and family paints a picture of your relationship as a parade of wrongs being done to you and you wonder why no one can understand why you're with him! You wouldn't want to be with the guy that you've described to them either!

Additionally, you can't give *all* the deets to your girlfriends, no matter how badly you may want to. First, that guy may eventually become a larger and more permanent part of your life (if you stop running your mouth!), and so you don't want everybody knowing how often you're having sex and which positions it's in and especially whether his "package" is large or small. It's a challenging thing to restrain yourself, but you have to. Talk to the girls when there's an action that can be taken to improve your situation, but whatever you do, do not vent! That is leading you down the path to being single Girlfriend! The more people that have details, the more people that you have to manage in the course of your relationship. For every person you tell, that's one more opinion to wade through as important decisions need to be made. The closer you keep it to just the two of you, the more limber your relationship will be.

When it comes to wrongs done to you in a relationship, friends and family have memories like elephants. Girlfriend, you'll want to just move on because you've forgotten about it and suddenly your Uncle Joe brings the story up at a Holiday dinner because he heard it from your Aunt Sue who heard it from your mother. Keep your relationship details to yourself specifically for the purpose of limiting the number of people in your relationship. Remember that game "Telephone" we all used to play as kids? You tell one person something and the statement travels all the way around the circle until it gets back to you and by that time it has totally mutated into an entirely different phrase? I think that our teachers were trying to give us an early lesson to keep us from being single later in life. When it comes to your relationship, avoid that game Girlfriend! Limit what you tell your friends and family. That's less people you'll have to explain your decisions to later when you resume your post as president of your guy's fan club!

MIY Maybe your finances are a disaster.

Nobody wakes up knowing how to manage money. More than a few of the girlfriends get caught in the credit card shuffle. I mean, sometimes a girl just picks the shoes over the student loan payment. It's irresponsible, yes, but the reality is, it happens. Not all of us can be Suze Orman! That said, when you're in a relationship, and all is well, the discussion about finances could take you off-guard. Many of the men that I've talked to said that they would not marry a girl whose finances were in disarray. Dating is fine, but when combining lives, taking responsibility for the other person who is an economic sinkhole was just one thing too many.

One of my girlfriends asked me recently, "What if I'm dating a guy who is financially-minded and to date I've been less responsible? Is he going to dump me once he finds out about my financial situation?" Girlfriend, if this is you, you've got some work to do! If you're self-sufficient, then your financial situation should not be that prevalent while you're dating. I don't know what guy asks a girl for her credit score before asking for her phone number. That said, if things are progressing toward a long-term plan, your guy is going to want to know what your economic landscape looks like. He may not want the specifics of your credit score (although some guys actually do), but he will want to know how responsible you've been and what kind of collateral damage he would have to deal with by incorporating you into his life. Believe it or not, Girlfriend, if he does want to marry you, your credit and finances are going to matter! So, why don't you make this something that you're aware of now and a conversation you have early? Get a handle on what his financial expectations are for a partner and make a determination for yourself of whether or not you can meet them. Now is the perfect time to start working on addressing your financial issues, because they could be keeping you single!

Girlfriend to Girlfriend SUGGESTION

Girlfriend, I know that in all of your fabulousness, it's expensive to be you! If you've dug yourself into a financial hole, it is not too late to at minimum stop digging! That's the first step. In all seriousness, if you want to get married, unless your guy is literally sitting on a gold mine, neither he nor anybody else is going to want to wed a financial liability. It's just a pure and simple undesirable quality. Stop thinking it doesn't or won't matter! It does and will keep you single! Start that conversation with your guy early. Find out what his expectations are. Don't let your economic landscape change the trajectory of your relationship. If you know that you have work to do to clean some things up, what are you waiting for?

MIY Maybe you're not committed to making the relationships that you do have work.

Speaking of expensive tastes, Girlfriend, let's imagine that you and I go shopping for a new outfit for fall. We want to combine jeans, a cute top and a blazer, all so that we can best show off the new boots we picked up on sale last week, ok? So, we go into the store and each of us pick up three possible sets that might work and go into the fitting room. You try on your first outfit and I try on mine. You come out of the dressing room wearing the top, jeans and blazer and look fabulous. I come out of the fitting room with one top and one blazer on one arm, another top and blazer on the other arm and a different pair of jeans on each leg. You're looking at me crazy, right? Why? Because I was supposed to try the *whole* outfit on at one time to see if it worked for me. Not part of one outfit and part of another. Doing that doesn't give you or I any idea of what either outfit even remotely looks like does it? What a waste of time, agreed?

So, Girlfriend, how does this apply to dating? Well, let's say you met a guy that you like. He's cool, but you don't step all the way into the relationship because you don't know that you're completely ready to give up what might be coming around the corner, or in fact, the schmuck that you're already seeing. Well, Girlfriend, doing that is tantamount to you trying on a bunch of different outfits all at the same time! You have to step fully into a relationship to know if it is truly going to work for you and your guy or not. You've got to put your heart on the line, even if being with one person might put you in jeopardy of your heart getting broken! That's what the girlfriends are for – to pick up the pieces and put you back together!

You're also not stepping all the way into a relationship if you date a guy only while things are perfect and then run at the first sign of something you don't like. Girlfriend, I'll be the first to admit, this is one of my biggest troubles. I will date a guy, and then, the first indication of a potential problem, even if still benign, I head towards the nearest exit. I am certainly not as willing as I should be to work through inevitable bumps in the road - in part, because I am afraid of getting hurt and in part because I just don't want to deal with it. Well, Girlfriend, I've let some pretty good guys go this way - all because of my own ignorance, thinking that there could ever be a perfect guy, and not wanting to push to try to work through issues.

If I'm totally honest with you, deep down, the feeling persists that every relationship is so fragile. I constantly fight the thought that bringing up the least little thing I don't like will cause the guy to leave me immediately! It is a struggle, but I'm starting to realize that most relationships are a little stronger than that, Girlfriend! The first time that I found the courage to bring up a concern to a guy that I was dating, I was shocked, absolutely shocked that after some calm and honest discussion, he understood where I was coming from and actually agreed to address the issue! And he really did! No one, married, dating or single has told me that relationships don't take an enormous amount of work. They present good times and bad. And no man (or woman) comes to a relationship perfect and complete. There's always room to grow - together.

Don't sell yourself short in the relationships that you do have. Put the whole outfit on, as I would say. Step into the relationship with your guy with both feet (and both eyes open, of course) and make your evaluation from that position. Don't hedge if you don't need to. If he's 100% there with you, then be 100% there with him. It could be that the relationship "fitting room" is keeping you single, Girlfriend!

If You're Essentially Perfect & It's Still Not Working, Maybe It's Him...

Girlfriend, there is more than a slight dose of facetiousness in this last chapter title. The truth is, no one is perfect and in many instances of a relationship not working, the guy is undeniably in some way at fault. There are countless unbelievably lame men who have managed to capture the hearts and minds of incredible women and of course, one of those women might be you! If that is the case, hopefully you will find the strength, courage and true awareness of your own value and demand better for yourself!

My intention for this last and final bit is to give a summary of what I hope that you take away from this book.

Like I said at the very beginning, not everything here will apply to you now. Maybe some of the issues you've already worked through in your past; maybe some you've never encountered. That's great, Congratulations. But for *all of us*, several of the circumstances, thoughts, mindsets and obstacles outlined in this book have applied, continue to apply and most of all, are keeping us single.

Not being single is an ongoing and active process of self-exploration, dealing with internal issues, tackling conflict and constantly striving to improve ourselves on the path of self-fulfillment. Perhaps, as you've read this book, you've noted sections that you'd like to revisit, highlighted topics to bring up with your girlfriends and action items for you and your interaction with your guy (your guy now, or your guy to come). Aside from the notes and the bookmarks, the primary take-away for you, my single Girlfriend, should be *hope*.

It is my deepest desire and wish that every girlfriend reading this book realizes that she has the power to control her happiness. Being single is not just some freakish state of existence that's far beyond her control. Nor is it just something to lament in the company of your fellow single girlfriends. It is a time of self-exploration and change; a time of development and internal progress, a time of experimentation and discovery that can only happen when you're alone and without distraction. Holding the highest expectation for your next best relationship around the corner will keep you in the state of mind to make the most of this temporary period.

I'll be the first to admit the "all men are dogs" conversation is fun. It's a great topic over drinks and it's much easier to shift the burden of successful relationships and the blame for those that failed to the opposite sex. It's fun until it becomes sad. Sad is the realization that if it really is them, then there's nothing you can do about it. Rather than wasting your breath on fruitless venting, all of that magnificent girlfriend energy and intelligence could be re-directed into each one of you helping the other to become a better woman. You *can* make the decision to do that, Girlfriend, but the choice is *entirely* yours.

As my parting note, I want to remind you that you are **FABULOUS**! You are a wonderful, unique, intelligent, beautiful, interesting creature that was only made once. Treat yourself as the true prize that you are. As long as you continue to work on yourself and hold on to your Standards, your dating landscape will change and so will your options. And yes, there are a million and one guys out there that are not deserving of you or your attention. This book is not about them. This book is about you and how to shift your focus and attention to the men that are deserving. Occasionally you will encounter a true and total loser, but if you know yourself, meaning who you truly are and what you're worth, he'll just be a passer-by instead of the "dog" that you're dishing to your girlfriends about.

I hate goodbyes, so I won't make this one. I invite you to continue our conversation on my website, via email or by leaving me a message. We'll keep talking, I'll keep writing and most of all, I'll keep wishing you, my Girlfriend best of luck in your new journey to happier dating and more fulfilling relationships!

Guide for Girlfriends

HOW TO HOST A PITY-LESS PARTY

So, Girlfriend, it's time to change the conversation about the men-folk! Next time you get together with the girlfriends, only spend half the time on "them," meaning the boys. Make this next conversation about you! Look, it is easy to start the typical happy-hour pity party. We've all done it a million times before. We get together as girlfriends and we could be talking about any topic under the sun and inevitably no matter what else we have to discuss, no matter who did what to whom, no matter what sales there are this week at our collective favorite store, we will ultimately wind up discussing relationships. Guaranteed. And unless you and your girlfriends are all from another planet (one I'd like to visit, mind you), that conversation is going to center on what men have done wrong recently that's got one or more of the girlfriends vexed.

Here's where you need to press pause. You, Girlfriend, are now armed with additional information that can change the conversation to something that is just as interesting, but now with a potentially positive outcome. Instead of getting together with the girls and ending the conversation on a note that we all already knew (*i.e.*, *some* men suck), you might be able to leave the conversation with some things to think about that you or your girlfriends personally can work on. Girlfriend, let me tell you, I did the research and wrote the book, and I'm still revisiting and revising quite a few things that I do! Believe me when I say that we *all* have work to do.

So with the objective of positive personal advancement, here are some suggestions to help turn what you've learned in this book into a pity-less party!

Grab some drinks (I prefer champagne, but martinis will do just nicely). I've included my mother's "Get Handed Lemons, Make Lemon Drop Martinis" recipe.

Before the conversation even heads in the direction of "men suck," let the girlfriends know that have something else to talk about. Have some of the MIY Topics in mind. If helpful, write some of the premises on 3"x5" cards (e.g, "Maybe you don't know what you want," "Maybe you're selfish," etc.) and bring them with you with a few relevant notes jotted on the back of each one.

Throw out a premise and invite the girlfriends to discuss individually if it applies to them. You might have to be the courageous one and go first. Girlfriend, you've already been thinking about it, so give it a go!

Make sure that you and the girlfriends decide that the pity-less party is a judgment free zone, and like Vegas, what goes on there, stays there. There can be no girlfriend-on-girlfriend violence (or silent treatment) for things said at the pity-less party. This is a key point. While the girlfriends might make personal statements about each other, it is not a condemnation, just something to think about as a possible area of improvement (if this point is an issue, bring up "Maybe you don't listen" – it should change the perspectives a bit).

Make sure that all the girls pick a take-away point for future reflection and discussion.

And of course Girlfriend, if you're drinking, drink responsibly!

Get Handed Lemons, Make Lemon Drop Martinis

3 oz	Lemonchello Creme (you can use Lemonchello liqueur, but my mom swears this stuff is the best!)
1.5 oz	Ruby Red Grapefruit Vodka
1.5 oz	Fresh Lemon Juice
1 tsp	Confectioner's Sugar
.5 oz	Fresh Grapefruit Juice (optional)

Combine ingredients in a martini shaker with ice. Cover and shake shake shake it Girlfriend! This recipe makes just one martini, so rinse and repeat!

Guide for Girlfriends

WHEN IT'S TIME TO HAVE A FRIENDTERVENTION

Sometimes one of the girlfriends can fall too far down the relationship rabbit hole. It's at that time that your girlfriend services are most needed to pull her up before she becomes lost in her bad relationship vortex. Without getting too specific, the bad relationship vortex can occur when a fellow girlfriend is in or out of a relationship, and quite frankly, most often occurs when she's not in one. A girlfriend in a bad relationship vortex may have given up on meeting guys, may be running all the right guys off, or may be insistent on dating the wrong guy over and over again (including those that are married or otherwise unavailable, abusive or undesirable or just flat-out mooching losers) and is headed quickly down a path that will result in her sure unending misery. If you've read this book and successfully identified your own issues, you'll probably start to identify the same issues in one or more of your girlfriends. If there's one in particular that's teetering dangerously close to the edge of no-return, in some form or fashion, you're going to want to have some type of friendtervention. Here are my suggestions:

Rules for a Friendtervention

Only include the girlfriend's closest friends. Make sure that you're all on the same page with the same objective.

Don't attack the girlfriend. Just ask her what she's feeling and if she thinks that she'd like things to change.

Gently broach the subject with examples of a few things that she might be doing that are causing her chronic singledom. Use specific facts, not statements that start with "I think."

Don't expect radical change at the beginning. Be willing to accept if she doesn't want to change. If she does want to change, be ready with suggestions for small steps that she can take.

Commit to some sort of follow up support. Shift the focus of "men suck" conversations to identifying issues that you have control over. That means self-analysis rather than external observations.

Guide for Girlfriends
FURTHER READING

Working on Yourself

- ***The Road Less Traveled*** **by M. Scott Peck**

  This book deals with all forms of love, including loving yourself. It helped me go from breakup to breakthrough on more than one occasion.

- ***Calling in the One*** **by Katherine Woodward Thomas**

  This book is more of a workbook, and is a prescribed course to be followed over a 7 week period. It is intense and filled with insight, but girlfriends should be prepared for the commitment to do the work which includes journaling and several projects as part of the recommended activities. That said, if you stick with it, it is like two years of therapy condensed.

- ***In the Meantime*** **by Inyala Vanzant**

  This book is filled with inspiration and encouragement, meant for the in-between time situations presented by life challenges in the quest for love. Part spiritual, part common-sense, the journey with Inyala is a healing one.

- ***The Four Agreements* by Don Miguel Ruiz**

  This book is a quick read, but is packed with powerful information. While it draws upon ancient Toltec wisdom to address successful interpersonal interactions, the approach centers largely on mastery of self and self love.

- ***Creative Visualization* by Shakti Gaiwan**

  If you need help seeing it and believing it, this book is a good tool. Shakti Gaiwan explains how to use what she calls "creative visualization" to help you in achieving your life goals.

What He's Thinking

- ***He's Just Not That Into You* by Greg Behrendt & Liz Tuccillo**

  This contemporary classic is not just a movie, it's a favorite phrase when things just aren't going right with your guy. It's definitely the reality check you may need when you find yourself wondering what he's thinking when he doesn't call, doesn't ask you out and generally doesn't act like he's interested.

- ***Act Like a Lady, Think Like a Man* by Steve Harvey**

  In contrast, this bestselling book explains how a man acts when he is into you. It gives good insight into the "language of man" in words and in action. My personal favorites are the questions that the book recommends that you ask as well as the 90-day rule.

Getting Out There

- ***Find a Husband After 35* by Rachael Greenwald**

  Despite the title of this book, I think that it's actually appropriate for single girlfriends of any age. Why wait until you're 35+ to get proactive about dating and finding a mate? This book has excellent suggestions for online dating, including setting up compelling profiles and making effective searches. The author cleverly uses the marketing tactics that she learned in business school to apply to women who are looking to find their guy.

- ***Become Your Own Matchmaker* by Patti Stanger**

  Written by the "Millionaire Matchmaker" herself, this book has some "no holds barred" advice on how to get a guy. She details where to meet eligible men and gives prescriptions for navigating the beginning of a new relationship. My favorite part of this book is the advice for setting up your online dating profile and general strategies for new ways of meeting the men-folk.

- ***All the Rules* by Ellen Fein and Sherrie Schneider**

  This is the old-school approach to getting a guy to like you. It's a prescription for behavior, neatly outlined in a list of do's and don'ts for contemporary women. It's good information, but focuses more on the what than the why.

- ***Art of Seduction*** **by Robert Greene**

  This is a well-written and highly-complex analysis of the different mechanisms of seduction from a historical perspective. More for entertainment and information than prescriptive application, this book provides great insight if you're wondering what captivating forces have entrapped the minds of even the most powerful of men.

Successful Relationships

- ***Art of Loving*** **by Erich Fromm**

  I most highly recommend this beautiful book that delves into the theory of love from a philosophical perspective. A very worthwhile discussion of love as an activity rather than a passive experience. When you're ready to take your thoughts of love and relationships to another level, this is the book to turn to. It's a relatively quick read, but it is packed with profound revelations.

- ***The Conversation*** **by Hill Harper**

  While primarily intended for African-American audiences, this book delves into the reasons behind the failings in romantic couplings between men and women and what can be done to mend the fences, a concept that can be applicable to people of all races. It is well-written and may help with further understanding different perspectives on relationships and their short-comings. To be looked at as an insightful conversation with a solid male friend.

- ***The Five Love Languages* by Gary Chapman**

This book centers primarily on communication between two people in a relationship. Since lack of communication is one of the primary causes of relationship failure, this could very well be an extremely important book. The central concept is that people tend to speak different "love languages" meaning that they understand love as expressed to them in a certain way. This book describes what those ways are and how to make more effective translations of your feelings of love to the person that you're with. A quick read and very insightful.

www.ingramcontent.com/pod-product-compliance
Lightning Source LLC
Chambersburg PA
CBHW071940090426
42740CB00011B/1758
9780981792200